East of Paris

Sketches in the Gâtinais, Bourbonnais, and Champagne

Matilda Betham-Edwards

Alpha Editions

This edition published in 2021

ISBN : 9789354548048

Design and Setting By
Alpha Editions
www.alphaedis.com
Email - info@alphaedis.com

As per information held with us this book is in Public Domain.
This book is a reproduction of an important historical work. Alpha Editions
uses the best technology to reproduce historical work in the same manner
it was first published to preserve its original nature. Any marks or number
seen are left intentionally to preserve its true form.

Contents

INTRODUCTORY	- 1 -
CHAPTER I MELUN	- 3 -
CHAPTER II MORET-SUR-LOING	- 6 -
CHAPTER III BOURRON	- 11 -
CHAPTER IV BOURRON—continued.	- 16 -
CHAPTER V BOURRON—continued.	- 20 -
CHAPTER VI LARCHANT	- 25 -
CHAPTER VII RECLOSES.	- 29 -
CHAPTER VIII NEMOURS.	- 33 -
CHAPTER IX LA CHARITÉ-SUR-LOIRE.	- 36 -
CHAPTER X POUGUES.	- 40 -
CHAPTER XI NEVERS AND MOULINS.	- 44 -
CHAPTER XII SOUVIGNY AND SENS.	- 53 -
CHAPTER XIII ARCIS-SUR-AUBE.	- 59 -
CHAPTER XIV ARCIS-SUR-AUBE—(continued).	- 64 -
CHAPTER XV RHEIMS.	- 68 -
CHAPTER XVI RHEIMS—(continued).	- 72 -
CHAPTER XVII SOULAINES AND BAR-SUR-AUBE.	- 78 -
CHAPTER XVIII ST. JEAN DE LOSNE.	- 86 -

CHAPTER XIX NANCY. - 90 -

CHAPTER XX IN GERMANISED LORRAINE. - 94 -

CHAPTER XXI IN GERMANISED ALSACE. - 101 -

INTRODUCTORY

I here propose to zig-zag with my readers through regions of Eastern France not described in any of my former works. The marvels of French travel, no more than the *chefs-d'oeuvre* of French literature, are unlimited. Short of saluting the tricolour on Mont Blanc, or of echoing the Marseillaise four hundred and odd feet underground in the cave of Padirac, I think I may fairly say that I have exhausted France as a wonder-horn. But quiet beauties and homely graces have also their seduction, just as we turn with a sense of relief from "Notre Dame de Paris" or "Le Père Goriot," to a domestic story by Rod or Theuriet, so the sweet little valley of the Loing refreshes after the awful Pass of Gavarni, and soothing to the ear is the gentle flow of its waters after the thundering Rhône. Majestic is the panorama spread before our eyes as we picnic on the Puy de Dôme. More fondly still my memory clings to many a narrower perspective, the view of my beloved Dijon from its vine-clad hills or of Autun as approached from Pré Charmoy, to me, the so familiar home of the late Philip Gilbert Hamerton. If, however, the natural marvels of France, like those of any other country, can be catalogued, French scenery itself offers inexhaustible variety. And so, having visited, re-visited, and re-visited again this splendid hexagon on the European map, I yet find in the choice of holiday resorts a veritable *embarras de richesses*. And many of the spots here described will, I have no doubt, be as new to my readers as they have been to myself—*Larchant* with its noble tower rising from the plain, recalling the still nobler ruin of Tclemcen on the borders of the Sahara—*Recloses* with its pictorial interiors and grand promontory overlooking a panorama of forest, sombre purplish green ocean unflecked by a single sail—*Moret* with its twin water-ways, one hardly knows which of the two being the more attractive—*Nemours*, favourite haunt of Balzac, memorialized in "Ursule Mirouët"—*La Charité*, from whose old-world dwellings you may throw pebbles into the broad blue Loire—*Pougues*, the prettiest place with the ugliest name, frequented by Mme. de Sévigné and valetudinarians of the Valois race generations before her time—*Souvigny*, cradle of the Bourbons, now one vast congeries of abbatial ruins—*Arcis-sur-Aube*, the sweet riverside home of Danton—its near neighbour, *Bar-sur-Aube*, connected with a bitterer enemy of Marie Antoinette than the great revolutionary himself, the infamous machinator of the Diamond Necklace. These are a few of the sweet nooks and corners to which of late years I have returned again and again, ever finding "harbour and good company." And these journeys, I should rather say visits, East of Paris led me once more to that sad yearning France beyond the frontier, to homes as French, to hearts as devoted to the motherland as when I first visited the annexed provinces twenty years ago!

CHAPTER I
MELUN

Scores upon scores of times had I steamed past Melun in the Dijon express, ever eyeing the place wistfully, ever too hurried, perhaps too lazy, to make a halt. Not until September last did I carry out a long cherished intention. It is unpardonable to pass and re-pass any French town without alighting for at least an hour's stroll!

Melun, capital of the ancient Gatinais, now chef-lieu of the Department of Seine and Marne, well deserves a visit. Pretty as Melun looks from the railway it is prettier still on nearer approach. The Seine here makes a loop, twice curling round the town with loving embrace, its walls and old world houses to-day mirrored in the crystal-clear river. Like every other French town, small or great, Melun possesses its outer ring of shady walks, boulevards lying beyond the river-side quarters. The place has a busy, prosperous, almost metropolitan look, after the village just left. {Footnote: For symmetry's sake I begin these records at Melun, although I halted at the place on my way from my third sojourn at Bourron.} The big, bustling Hotel du Grand Monarque too, with its brisk, obliging landlady, invited a stay. Dr. Johnson, perhaps the wittiest if the completest John Bull who ever lived, was not far wrong when he glorified the inn. "Nothing contrived by man," he said, "has produced so much happiness (relaxation were surely the better word?) as a good tavern." Do we not all, to quote Falstaff, "take our ease at our inn," under its roof throwing off daily cares, assuming a holiday mood?

A survey of the yard awoke another train of reflections. It really seems as if the invention of the motor car were bringing back ante-railway days for the tourist and the travelling world, recalling family coach and post-chaise. The place was crowded with motor cars of all shapes and sizes, some of these were plain, shabby gigs and carts of commercial travellers, others, landaus, waggonettes and victorias of rich folks seeing the world in their own carriage as their ancestors had done generations before; one turn-out suggested royalty or a Rothschild, I was about to say, rather I should name a Chicago store-keeper, since American millionaires are the Haroun-el-Raschids of the twentieth century. This last was a sumptuously fitted up carriage having a seat behind for servants, accommodating eight persons in all. There was also a huge box for luggage. It would be interesting to know how much petroleum, electricity, or alcohol such a vehicle would consume in a day. The manufacture of motor cars must be a very flourishing business in France, next, I should say, to that of bicycles. Of these also there was a goodly supply in the entrance hall of the inn, and the impetus given to travel by both motor car and bicycle was here self-evident. The Hotel du Grand Monarque literally swarmed with tourists, one and all French folks taking their ease at their inn. And our neighbours do not take their pleasure solemnly after the manner of the less impressionable English. Stay-at-home as they have hitherto been, home-loving as they essentially are, the atmosphere of an inn, the aroma of a holiday, fill the Frenchman's cup of hilarity to overflowing, rendering gayer the gayest.

The invention and rapidly spreading use of the motor car in France shows the French character under its revolutionary aspect, yet no people on the face of the earth are in many respects so conservative. We English folks want a new "Where is it?" for social purposes every year, the majority of our friends and acquaintances changing their houses almost as often as milliners and tailors change the fashion in bonnets and coats. A single address book for France supplies a life-time. The explanation is obvious. For the most part we live in other folks' houses whilst French folks, the military and official world excepted, occupy their own. Revisit provincial gentry or well-to-do bourgeoisie after an interval of a quarter of a century, you always find them where they were. Interiors show no more change than the pyramids of Egypt. Not so much as sixpence has been laid out upon new carpets or curtains. Could grandsires and granddames return to life like the Sleeping Beauty, they would find that the world had stood still during their slumber.

Melun possesses perhaps one of the few statues that may not be called superfluous, and I confess I had been attracted thither rather by memories of its greatest son than by its picturesque scenery and fine old churches. The first translator of Plutarch into his native tongue was born here, and as we should expect, has been worthily commemorated by his fellow citizens. A most charming statue of Amyot stands in front of the grey, turreted

Hôtel de Ville. In sixteenth century doctoral dress, loose flowing robes and square flat cap, sits the great scholiast, as intently absorbed in his book as St. Jerome in the exquisite canvas of our own National Gallery.

Behind the Hôtel de Ville an opening shows a small, beautifully kept flower garden, just now a blaze of petunias, zinnias, and a second crop of roses. Long I lingered before this noble monument, one only of the many raised to Amyot's memory, of whom Montaigne wrote:—

"Ignoramuses that we are, we should all have been lost, had not this book (the translation of Plutarch) dragged us out of the mire; thanks to it, we now venture to write and to discourse."

And musing on the scholar and his kindred, a favourite line of Browning's came into my mind—

"This man decided not to live but to know."

Indeed the whole of "A Grammarian's Funeral" were here appropriate. Is it not men after this type of whom we feel

"Our low life was the level's and the night's.

He's for the morning"?

To my surprise I found the church of St. Aspais locked. A courteous hair-dresser thereupon told me that all churches in Melun were closed from noon till half past one, but that, as noon had only just struck, if I were brisk I might possibly catch the sacristan. After a pretty hot chase I succeeded in finding a deaf, decrepit, dingy old man who showed me round the church, although evidently very impatient for his mid-day meal. He informed me that this closing of churches at Melun had been necessitated of late years by a series of robberies. From twelve till half past one o'clock no worshippers are present as a rule, hence the thieves' opportunity. Unfortunately marauders do not strip beautiful interiors of the tinselly gew-gaws that so often deface them; in this respect, however, St. Aspais being comparatively an exception. Alike within and without the proportions are magnificent, and the old stained glass is not marred by modern crudities. I do not here by any means exhaust the sights of this ancient town, from which, by the way, Barbizon is now reached in twenty minutes, an electric tramway plying regularly between Melun and that famous art pilgrimage.

CHAPTER II
MORET-SUR-LOING

The valley of the Loing abounds in captivating spots, Moret-sur-Loing bearing the palm. Over the ancient town, bird-like broods a majestic church, as out-spread wings its wide expanse of roof, while below by translucent depths and foliage richly varied, stretch quarters old and new, the canal intersecting the river at right angles. Lovely as is the river on which all who choose may spend long summer days, the canal to my thinking is lovelier still. Straight as an arrow it saunters between avenues of poplar, the lights and shadows of wood and water, the sunburnt, stalwart barge folk, their huge gondoliers affording endless pictures. Hard as is undoubtedly the life of the rope tower, rude as may appear this amphibious existence, there are cheerful sides to the picture. Many of these floating habitations possess a fireside nook cosy as that of a Parisian concierge, I was never tired of strolling along the canal and watching the barge folk. One day a friend and myself found a large barge laden with coal at the head of the canal, the huge dark framework and its sombre burden lighted up with touches of grace and colour. At the farther end of the vessel was hung a cage of canaries, at the other end was a stand of pot-flowers, geraniums and petunias in full bloom and all the more brilliant by virtue of contrast. A neighbour of the bargeman, a bright, intelligent woman, brown as a gipsy but well-spoken and of tidy appearance, invited us to enter. Imagine the neatest, prettiest little room in the world, parlour, bedchamber and kitchen in one, every object so placed as to make the most of available space. On a small side-table—and of course under such circumstances each article must be sizable—stood a sewing machine, in the corner was a bedstead with exquisitely clean bedding, in another a tiny cooking stove. Vases of flowers, framed pictures and ornamental quicksilver balls had been found place for, this bargewoman's home aptly illustrating Shakespeare's adage—"Order gives all things view." The brisk, weather-beaten mistress now came up, no little gratified by our interest and our praises.

"You ladies would perhaps like to make a little journey with me?" she asked, "nothing easier, we start to-morrow morning at six o'clock for Nevers, you could take the train back."

Never perhaps in our lives had myself and my companion received an invitation so out of the way, so bewilderingly tempting! And we felt too, with a pang, that never again in all probability should we receive such another. But on this especial day we were not staying at Moret, only running over for the afternoon from our headquarters at Bourron. Acceptance was thus hemmed round with small impediments. And by way of consolation, next morning the glorious weather broke. A downpour recalling our own lakeland would anyhow have kept us ashore.

"Another time then!" had said the kind hostess of the barge at parting. She seemed as sorry as ourselves that the little project she had mooted so cordially could not be carried out.

The Loing canal joins the Seine at Saint Mammes, a few kilomètres lower down, continuing its course of thirty kilomètres to Bleneau in the Nièvre. Canal life in Eastern France is a characteristic feature, the whole region being intersected by a network of waterways, those *chemins qui marchent*, or walking roads as Michelet picturesquely calls them. And strolling on the banks of the canal here you may be startled by an astonishing sight, you see folks walking, or apparently walking, on water. Standing bolt upright on a tiny raft, carefully maintaining their balance, country people are towed from one side to the other.

These suburban and riverside quarters are full of charm. The soft reds and browns of the houses, the old-world architecture and romantic sites, tempt an artist at every turn. And all in love with a Venetian existence may here find it nearer home.

A few villas let furnished during the summer months have little lawns winding down to the water's edge and a boat moored alongside. Thus their happy inmates can spend hot, lazy days on the river.

Turning our backs on the canal, by way of ivy-mantled walls, ancient mills and tumbledown houses, we reach the Porte du Pont or Gate of the Bridge. With other towns of the period, Moret was fortified. The girdle of walls is broken and dilapidated, whilst firm as when erected in the fourteenth century still stand the city gates.

Of the two the Porte du Pont is the least imposing and ornamental, but it possesses a horrifying interest. In an upper storey is preserved one of those man-cages said to have been invented for the gratification of Louis XI, that strange tyrant to whose ears were equally acceptable the shrieks of his tortured victims and the apt repartee of ready-witted subjects.

"How much do you earn a day?" he once asked a little scullion, as incognito he entered the royal kitchen.

"By God's grace as much as the King," replied the lad; "I earn my bread and he can do no more."

So pleased was the King with this saying that it made the speaker's fortune.

We climb two flights of dark, narrow stone stairs reaching a bare chamber having small apertures, enlargements of the mere slits formerly admitting light and air. The man-cage occupies one corner. It is made of stout oaken ribs strongly bound together with iron, its proportions just allowing the captive to lie down at full length and take a turn of two or three steps. De Commines tells us that the cage invented by Cardinal Balue, and in which he languished for eleven years, was narrower still. An average sized man could not stand therein upright.

The bolts and bars are still in perfect order. Nothing more brings home to us the abomination of the whole thing than to see the official draw these Brobdingnagian bolts and turn these gigantic keys. The locksmith's art was but too well understood in those days. By whom and for whom this living tomb was made or brought hither local records do not say.

From a stage higher up a magnificent panorama is obtained, Moret, old and new, set round with the green and the blue, its greenery and bright river, far away its noble aqueduct, further still looking eastward the valley of the Loing spread out as a map, the dark ramparts of Fontainebleau forest half framing the scene.

The town itself is a trifle unsavoury and unswept. Municipal authorities seem particularly stingy in the matter of brooms, brushes and water-carts. Such little disagreeables must not prevent the traveller from exploring every corner. But the real, the primary attraction of Moret lies less in its historic monuments and antiquated streets than in its *chemins qui marchent*, its ever reposeful water-ways. Like most French towns Moret is linked with English history. Its fine old church was consecrated by Thomas à-Becket in 1166. Three hundred years later the town was taken by Henry V., and re-taken by Charles VII. a decade after. Not long since five hundred skulls supposed to have been those of English prisoners were unearthed here; as they were all found massed together, the theory is that the entire number had surrendered and been summarily decapitated, methods of warfare that have apparently found advocates in our own day.

Most visitors to Paris will have had pointed out to them the so-called "Maison François Premier" on the Cour La Reine. This richly ornate and graceful specimen of Renaissance architecture formerly stood at Moret, and bit by bit was removed to the capital in 1820. A spiral stone staircase and several fragments of heraldic sculpture were left behind. Badly placed as the house was here, it seems a thousand pities that Moret should have thus been robbed of an architectural gem Paris could well have spared.

My first stay at Moret three years ago lasted several weeks. I had joined friends occupying a pretty little furnished house belonging to the officiating Mayor. We lived after simplest fashion but to our hearts' content. One of those indescribably obliging women of all work, came every day to cook, clean and wait on us. Most of our meals were taken among our flower beds and raspberry bushes. The only drawback to enjoyment may at first sight appear unworthy of mention, but it was not so. We had no latchkey. Now as every-one of all work knows, they are constantly popping in and out of doors, one moment they are off to market, the next to warm up their husbands' soup, and so on and so on. As for ourselves, were we not at Moret on purpose to be perpetually running about also? Thus it happened that somebody or other was always being locked out or locked in; either Monsieur finding the household abroad had pocketed the key and instead of returning in ten minutes' time had lighted upon a subject he must absolutely sketch then and there; or Madame could not get through her shopping as expeditiously as she had hoped; or their guest returned from her walk long before she was due; what with one miscalculation and another, now one of us had to knock at a neighbour's door, now another effected an entrance by means of a ladder, and now the key would be wholly missing and for the time being we were roofless, as if burnt out of house and home. Sometimes we were locked in, sometimes we were locked out, a current "Open Sesame" we never had.

But no "regrettable incidents" marred a delightful holiday. Imbroglios such as these only leave memories to smile at, and add zest to recollection.

CHAPTER III
BOURRON

Two years ago some Anglo-French friends joyfully announced their acquisition of a delightful little property adjoining Fontainebleau forest. "Come and see for yourself," they wrote, "we are sure that you will be charmed with our purchase!" A little later I journeyed to Bourron, half an hour from Moret on the Bourbonnais line, on arriving hardly less disconcerted than Mrs. Primrose by the gross of green spectacles. No trim, green verandahed villa, no inviting vine-trellised walk, no luxuriant vegetable garden or brilliant flower beds greeted my eyes; instead, dilapidated walls, abutting on these a peasant's cottage, and in front an acre or two of bare dusty field! My friends had indeed become the owners of a dismantled bakery and its appurtenances, to the uninitiated as unpromising a domain as could well be imagined. But I discovered that the purchasers were wiser in their generation than myself. Noticing my crestfallen look they had said:—

"Only wait till next year, and you will see what a bargain we have made. You will find us admirably housed and feasting on peaches and grapes."

True enough, twelve months later, I found a wonderful transformation. That a substantial dwelling now occupied the site of the dismantled bakery was no matter for surprise, the change out of doors seemed magical. Nothing could have looked more unpromising than that stretch of field, a mere bit of waste, your feet sinking into the sand as if you were crossing the desert. Now, the longed-for *tonnelle* or vine-covered way offered shade, petunias made a splendid show, choice roses scented the air, whilst the fruit and vegetables would have done credit to a market-gardener. Peaches and grapes ripened on the wall, big turnips and tomatoes brilliant as vermilion took care of themselves. It was not only a case of the wilderness made to blossom as the rose, but of the horn of plenty filled to overflowing, prize flowers, fruit and vegetables everywhere. For the soil hereabouts, if indeed soil it can be called, and the climate of Bourron, possess very rare and specific qualities. On this light, dry sand, or dust covering a substratum of rock, vegetation springs up all but unbidden, and when once above ground literally takes care of itself. As to climate, its excellence may be summed up in the epithet, anti-asthmatic. Although we are on the very hem of forty thousand acres of forest, the atmosphere is one of extraordinary dryness. Rain may fall in torrents throughout an entire day. The sandy soil is so thorough an absorbent that next morning the air will be as dry as usual.

This house reminded me of a tiny side door opening into some vast cathedral. We cross the threshold and find ourselves at once in the forest, in close proximity moreover to its least-known but not least majestic sites. We may turn either to right or left, gradually climbing a densely wooded headland. The first ascent lands us in an hour on the Redoute de Bourron, the second, occupying only half the time, on a spur of the forest offering a less famous but hardly less magnificent perspective, nothing to mar the picture as a whole, sunny plain, winding river and scattered townlings looking much as they must have done to Balzac when passing through three-quarters of a century ago.

This eastern verge of the Fontainebleau forest is of especial beauty; the frowning headlands seem set there as sentinels jealously guarding its integrity, on the watch against human encroachments, defying time and change and cataclysmal upheaval. Boldly stands out each wooded crag, the one confronting the rising, the other the sinking sun, behind both massed the world of forest, spread before them as a carpet, peaceful rural scenes.

I must now describe a spot, the name of which will probably be new to all excepting close students of Balzac. The great novelist loved the valley of the Loing almost as fondly as his native Touraine; and if these pastoral scenes did not inspire a *chef d'oeuvre*, they have thereby immensely gained in interest. "Ursule Mirouët," of which I shall have more to say further on, is not to be compared to such masterpieces as "Eugénie Grandet." But a leading incident of "Ursule Mirouët" occurs at Bourron—a sufficient reason for recalling the story here.

The beauty of our village, like the beauty of French women, to quote Michelet, "is made up of little nothings." There are a hundred and one pretty things to see but very few to describe. Who could wish it otherwise? Little nothings of an engaging kind better agree with us as daily fare than the seven wonders of the world. With forty thousand acres of forest at our doors we do not want M. Mattel's newly discovered underground river within reach as well.

From our garden we yet look upon scenes not of every day. Those sweeps of bluish-green foliage strikingly contrasted with the brilliant vine remind us that we are in France, and in a region with most others having its specialities. Asparagus, not literally but figuratively, nourishes the entire population of Bourron. Everyone here is a market gardener on his own account, and the cultivation of asparagus for the Paris markets is a leading feature of local commerce.

There is no more graceful foliage than that of this plant, and gratefully the eye rests upon these waves of delicate green under a blazing, grape-ripening sky. Making gold-green lines between are vines, a succession of asparagus beds and vineyards separating our village from its better known and more populous neighbour, Marlotte. In the opposite direction we see brown-roofed, white-walled houses surmounted by a pretty little spire. This is Bourron. To reach it we pass a double row of homesteads, rustic interiors of small farmer or market gardener, the one, as our French neighbours say, more picturesque than the other. Each, no matter how ill kept, is set off by an ornamental border, zinnias, begonias, roses and petunias as obviously showing signs of care and science. Oddly enough the finest display of flowers often adorns the least tidy premises. And oddly enough, rather perhaps as we should expect it, in not one, but in every respect, this French village is the exact opposite of its English counterpart. In England every tenant of a cottage pays rent, there, not an inhabitant, however poor, but sits under his own vine and his own fig-tree. In England the farmhouse faces the road and the premises lie behind. Here manure-heap, granary and pig styes open on the highway, the dwellings being at the back. In England a man's home, called his castle, is no more defended than the Bedouin's tent. Here at nightfall the small peasant proprietor is as securely entrenched within walls as a feudal baron in his moated château. In England ninety-nine householders out of a hundred are perpetually changing their domicile. Here folks live and die under the paternal roof that has sheltered generations. Nor does diversity end with circumstances and surroundings. As will be seen in another chapter, habits of life, modes of thought and standards of duty show contrasts equally marked.

Bourron possesses twelve hundred and odd souls, most of whom are peasants who make a living out of their small patrimony. Destined perhaps one day to rival its neighbour Marlotte in popularity—even to become a second Barbizon—it is as yet the sleepiest, most rustic retreat imaginable. The climate would appear to be not only anti-asthmatic but anti-everything in the shape of malady. Anyhow, if folks fall ill they have to send elsewhere for a doctor. Minor complaints—cuts, bruises and snake bites—are attended to by a Fontainebleau chemist. Every day we hear the horn of his messenger who cycles through the village calling for prescriptions and leaving drugs and draughts.

A post office, of course, Bourron possesses, but let no one imagine that a post office in out of the way country places implies a supply of postage stamps. English people are the greatest scribblers by post in the world, whilst our wiser French neighbours appear to be the laziest. An amusing dilemma had occurred here just before my arrival. One day my friends applied to the post office for stamps, but none were to be had for love or money. Off somebody cycled to Marlotte, which possesses not only a post and telegraph, but a money order office as well—same reply, next the adjoining village of Grez was visited and with no better result—"Supplies have not yet reached us from headquarters," said the third postmistress.

Perhaps instead of smiling contemptuously we should take a moral to heart. The amount of time, money, eyesight and handcraft expended among ourselves on letter writing so-called is simply appalling. Was it not Napoleon who said that all letters if left unanswered for a month answered themselves? Too many Englishwomen spend the greater portion of the day in what is no longer a delicate art, but mere time-killing, after the manner of patience, games of cards and similar pastimes.

Bourron is a most orderly village; within its precincts liberty is not allowed to degenerate into licence. As in summer-time folks are fond of spending their evenings abroad, a municipal law has enforced quiet after ten o'clock. Thus precisely on the stroke of ten, alike café, garden, private summer-house or doorstep are deserted, everyone betakes himself indoors, leaving his neighbours to enjoy unbroken repose. A most salutary by-law!

Would it were put in force throughout the length and breadth of France! At Chatouroux I have been kept awake all night by the gossip of a *sergeant de ville* and a lounger close to my window. At Tours, La Châtre and Bourges my fellow-traveller and myself could get no sleep on account of street revellers, whilst at how many other places have not holiday trips been spoiled by unquiet nights? All honour then to the aediles of dear little Bourron!

CHAPTER IV
BOURRON—*continued.*

Forty thousand acres of woodland at one's doors would seem a fact sufficiently suggestive; to particularize the attractions of Bourron after this statement were surely supererogation. Yet, for my own pleasure as much as for the use of my readers, I must jot down one or two especially persistent memories, impressions of solemnity, beauty and repose never to be effaced.

Of course it is only the cyclist who can realise such an immensity as the Fontainebleau forest. From end to end these vast sweeps are now intersected by splendid roads and by-roads. Old-fashioned folks, for whom the horseless vehicle came too late, can but envy wheelmen and wheelwomen as they skim through vista after vista, outstripping one's horse and carriage as a greyhound outstrips a decrepit poodle. On the other hand only inveterate loiterers, the Lazy Lawrences of travel, can appreciate the subtler beauties of this woodland world. There are certain sights and sounds not to be caught by hurried observers, evanescent aspects of cloud-land and tree-land, rock and undergrowth, passing notes of bird and insect, varied melodies, if we may so express it, of summer breeze and autumn wind—in fine, a dozen experiences enjoyed one day, not repeated on the next. The music of the forest is a quiet music and has to be listened for, hardly on the cyclist's ear falls the song or rather accompaniment of the grasshopper, "the Muse of the wayside," a French poet has so exquisitely apostrophized.

One's forest companion should be of a taciturn and contemplative turn. Only thus can we drink in the sense of such solitude and immensity; realizing to the full what indeed these words may mean, he may wander for hours without encountering a soul, very few birds are heard by the way, but the hum of the insect world, that dreamy go-between, hardly silence, hardly to be called noise, keeps us perpetual company, and our eyes must ever be open for beautiful little living things. Now a green and gold lizard flashes across a bit of grey rock, now a dragon-fly disports its sapphire wings amid the yellowing ferns or purple ling, butterflies, white, blue, and black and orange, flit hither and thither, whilst little beetles, blue as enamel beads, enliven the mossy undergrowth.

One pre-eminent charm indeed of the Fontainebleau forest is this wealth of undergrowth, bushes, brambles and ferns making a second lesser thicket on all sides. In sociable moods delightful it is to go a-blackberrying here. I am almost tempted to say that if you want to realise the lusciousness of a hedgerow dessert you must cater for yourself in these forty thousand acres of blackberry orchard.

But the foremost, the crowning excellence of Fontainebleau forest consists in its variety. France itself, the "splendid hexagon," with its mountains, rivers and plains, is hardly more varied than this vast area of rock and woodland. We can choose between sites, savage or idyllic, pastoral or grandiose, here finding a sunny glade, the very spot for a picnic, there break-neck declivities and gloomy chasms. The magnificent ruggedness of Alpine scenery is before our eyes, without the awfulness of snow-clad peaks or the blinding dazzle of glacier. In more than one place we could almost fancy that some mountain has been upheaved and split asunder, the clefts formed by these gigantic fragments being now filled with veteran trees.

The formation of the forest has puzzled geologists, to this day the origin of its rocky substratum remaining undetermined.

Within half an hour's stroll of Bourron lies the so-called "Mare aux Fées" or Fairies' Mere, as sweet a spot to boil one's kettle in as holiday makers can desire, at the same time affording the best possible illustration of what I have just insisted upon. For this favourite resort is in a certain sense microcosmic, giving in miniature those characteristics for which the forest is remarkable. Smooth and sunny as a garden plot is the open glade wherein we now halt for tea, and while the kettle boils we have time for a most suggestive bird's eye view. It is a little world that we survey from the borders of this rock-hemmed, forest-girt lake, one perspective after another with varying gradations of colour making us realize the many-featured, chequered area spread before us. From this coign of vantage are discerned alike the sterner and the more smiling beauties of the forest, rocky defiles, gloomy passes, sunlit lawns and mossy dells, scenery varied in itself and yet varying again with the passing hour and changing month. And such suggestion of almost infinite variety is not gained only from the Fairies' Mere. From a dozen points, not the same view but the same kind of view may be obtained, each differing from the other, except in charm and immensity. Within a walk of home also stands one of the numerous monuments scattered throughout the forest. The Croix de Saint Hérem, now a useful landmark for cyclists, has a curious history. It was erected in 1666 by a certain Marquis de Saint-Hérem, celebrated for his ugliness, and centuries later was the scene of the most extraordinary rendezvous on record. Here, in 1804, every detail having been theatrically arranged beforehand, took place the so-called chance meeting of Napoleon and Pope Pius VII. The Emperor had arranged a grand hunt for that day, and in hunting dress, his dogs at his heels, awaited the pontiff by the cross of Saint Hérem. As the pair lovingly embraced each other the Imperial horses ran away; this apparent escapade formed part of the programme, and Napoleon stepped into the Pope's carriage, seating himself on his visitor's, rather his prisoner's, right. A few years later another rencontre not without historic irony took place here. In 1816, Louis XVIII. received on this spot the future mother, so it was hoped, of French Kings, the adventurous Caroline of Naples, afterwards Duchesse de Berri.

The crosses monuments of the forest are usefully catalogued in local guide-books, and many have historic associations. The most interesting of these—readers will excuse the Irish bull—is a monument that may be said never to have existed!

The great Polish patriot Kosciusko spent the last fifteen years of his life in a hamlet near Nemours, and on his death the inhabitants of that and neighbouring villages projected a double memorial, in other words, a tiny chapel, the ruins of which are still seen near Episy, and a mound to be added to every year and to be called "La Montagne de Kosciusko," or Kosciusko's mountain. Particulars of this generous and romantic scheme are preserved in the archives of Montigny. The inauguration of the mound took place on the ninth of October 1836. To the sound of martial music, drums and cannon, the first layers of earth were deposited, men, women and children taking part in the proceedings. A year later no less than ten thousand French friends of Poland with mattock and spade added several feet to Kosciusko's mountain. But the celebration got noised abroad. Afraid of anti-Russian manifestations the government of Louis Philippe prohibited any further Polish fêtes. Thus it came about that, as I have said, the most interesting monument in the forest remains an idea. And all things considered, neither French nor English admirers of the exiled hero could to-day very well carve on the adjoining rock,

> *"And Freedom shrieked when Kosciusko fell."*

Some time or other the Russian Imperial pair may visit Fontainebleau, whilst an English tourist with *The Daily Mail* in his pocket would naturally and sheepishly look the other way.

Another half hour's stroll and we find ourselves in an atmosphere of art, fashion and sociability. Only a mile either of woodland, field path or high road separates Bourron from its more populous and highly popular neighbour, Marlotte. Here every house has an artist's north window, the road is alive with motor cars, you can even buy a newspaper! Marlotte possesses a big, I should say comfortable, hotel, is very cosmopolitan and very pretty. Anglo-French households here, as at Bourron, favour Anglo-French relations. In Marlotte drawing-rooms we are in France, but always with a pleasant reminder of England and of true English hospitality.

CHAPTER V
BOURRON—*continued.*

I will now say something about my numerous acquaintances at Bourron. After three summer holidays spent in this friendly little spot I can boast of a pretty large visiting list, the kind of list requiring no cards or ceremonious procedure. My hostess, a Frenchwoman, and myself used to drop in for a chat with this neighbour and that whenever we passed their way, always being cheerily welcomed and always pressed to stay a little longer.

The French peasant is the most laborious, at the same time the most leisurely, individual in the world. Urgent indeed must be those farming operations that prevent him from enjoying a talk. Conversation, interchange of ideas, give and take by word of mouth, are as necessary to the Frenchman's well-being as oxygen to his lungs.

"Man," writes Montesquieu, "is described as a sociable animal." From this point of view it appears to me that the Frenchman may be called more of a man than others; he is first and foremost a man, since he seems especially made for society.

Elsewhere the same great writer adds:—"You may see in Paris individuals who have enough to live upon for the rest of their days, yet they labour so arduously as to shorten their days, in order, as they say, to assure themselves of a livelihood." These two marked characteristics are as true of the French peasant now-a-days as of the polite society described in the "Lettres Persanes." In the eighteenth century cultivated people did little else but talk. Morning, noon and night, their epigrammatic tongues were busy. Conversation in historic salons became a fine art. There are no such literary côteries in our time. What with one excitement and another, the Parisian world chats but has no time for real conversation. Perhaps for *Gauloiseries*, true Gallic salt, we must now go to the unlettered, the sons of the soil, whose ancestors were boors when wit sparkled among their social superiors.

Here are one or two types illustrating both characteristics, excellent types in their way of the small peasant proprietor hereabouts, a class having no counterpart or approximation to a counterpart in England.

The first visit I describe was paid one evening to an old gardener whom I will call the Père A—. Bent partly with toil, partly with age, you would have at once supposed that his working days were well over, especially on learning his circumstances, for sole owner he was of the little domain to which he had now retired for the day. Of benevolent aspect, shrewd, every inch alive despite infirmities, he received his neighbour and her English guest with rustic but cordial urbanity, at once entering into conversation. With evident pride and pleasure he watched my glances at premises and garden, house and outbuildings ramshackle enough, even poverty-stricken to look at, here not an indication of comfortable circumstances much less of independent means; the bit of land half farm, half garden, however, was fairly well kept and of course productive.

"Yes, this dwelling is mine and the two hectares (four acres four hundred and odd feet), aye," he added self-complacently, "and I have a little money besides."

"Yet you live here all by yourself and still work for wages?" I asked. His reply was eminently characteristic. "I work for my children." These children he told me were two grown up sons, one of them being like himself a gardener, both having work. Thus in order to hoard up a little more for two able-bodied young men, here was a bent, aged man living penuriously and alone, his only companion being a beautiful and evidently much petted donkey. I ventured to express an English view of the matter, namely, the undesirability of encouraging idleness and self-indulgence in one's children by toiling and moiling for them in old age.

He nodded his head.

"You are right, all that you say is true, but so it is with me. I must work for my children."

And thus blindly are brought about the parricidal tragedies that Zola, Guy de Maupassant and other novelists have utilized in fiction, and with which we are familiarized in French criminal reports—parents and grandparents got rid of for the sake of their coveted hoardings.

Thus also are generated in the rich and leisured classes that intense selfishness of the rising generation so movingly portrayed in M. Hervieu's play, "La Course du Flambeau." No one who has witnessed Mme. Réjane's presentment of the adoring, disillusioned mother can ever forget it.

On leaving, the Père A—— presented us with grapes and pears, carefully selecting the finest for his English visitor.

At the gate I threw a Parthian dart.

"Don't work too hard," I said, whereupon came the burden of his song:

"One must work for one's children."

This good neighbour could neither read nor write, a quite exceptional case in these days. Our second visit was made to a person similarly situated, but belonging to a different order.

Madame B——, a widow, was also advanced in years and also lived by herself on her little property, consisting of walled-in cottage and outhouses, with straggling garden or rather orchard, garden and field in one.

This good woman is what country folks in these parts call rich. I have no doubt that an English farmeress in her circumstances would have the neatest little parlour, a tidy maid to wait upon her, and most likely take afternoon tea in a black silk gown. Our hostess here wore the dress of a poor but respectable working woman. Her interior was almost as bare and primitive as that of the Boer farmhouse in the Paris Exhibition. Although between six and seven o'clock, there was no sign whatever of preparation for an evening meal. Indeed on every side things looked poverty-stricken. Not a penny had evidently been spent upon kitchen or bedrooms for years and years, the brick floor of both being bare, the furniture having done duty for generations.

This "rentière," or person living upon independent means, did not match her sordid surroundings. Although toil-worn, tanned and wrinkled, her face "brown as the ribbed sea-sand," there was a certain refinement about look, speech and manner, distinguishing her from the good man her neighbour. After a little conversation I soon found out that she had literary tastes.

"Living alone and finding the winter evenings long I hire books from a lending library at Fontainebleau," she said.

I opened my eyes in amazement. Seldom indeed had I heard of a peasant proprietor in France caring for books, much less spending money upon them.

"And what do you read?" I asked.

"Anything I can get," was the reply. "Madame's husband," here she looked at my friend, "has kindly lent me several."

Among these I afterwards found had been Zola's "Rome" and "Le Désastre" by the brothers Margueritte.

Like the Père A—— she had married children and entertained precisely the same notion of parental duty. The few sous spent upon such beguilement of long winter nights were most likely economized by some little deprivation. There is something extremely pathetic in this patriarchal spirit, this uncompromising, ineradicable resolve to hand down a little patrimony not only intact but enlarged.

"Our peasants live too sordidly," observed a Frenchman to me a day or two later. "They carry thrift to the pitch of avarice and vice. Zola's 'La Terre' is not without foundation on fact."

And excellent as is the principle of forethought, invaluable as is the habit of laying by for a rainy day, I have at last come to the conclusion that of the two national weaknesses, French avarice and English lavishness and love of spending, the latter is more in accordance with progress and the spirit of the age.

In another part of the village we called upon a hale old body of seventy-seven, who not only lived alone and did everything for herself indoors but the entire work of a market garden, every inch of the two and a half acres being, of course, her own. Piled against an inner wall we saw a dozen or so faggots each weighing, we were told, half a hundredweight. Will it be believed that this old woman had picked up and carried from the forest on her back every one of these faggots? The poor, or rather those who will, are allowed to glean firewood in all the State forests of France. Let no tourist bestow a few sous upon aged men and women bearing home such treasure-trove! Quite possibly the dole may affront some owner of houses and lands.

As we inspected her garden, walls covered with fine grapes, tomatoes and melons, of splendid quality, to say nothing of vegetables in profusion, it seemed all the more difficult to reconcile facts so incongruous. Here was a market gardener on her own account, mistress of all she surveyed, glad as a gipsy to pick up sticks for winter use. But the burden of her story was the same:

"Il faut travailler pour ses enfants" (one must work for one's children), she said.

All these little farm-houses are so many homely fortresses, cottage and outhouses being securely walled in, a precaution necessary with aged, moneyed folks living absolutely alone.

A fourth visit was paid to a charming old Philémon and Baucis, the best possible specimens of their class. The husband lay in bed, ill of an incurable malady, and spotlessly white were his tasselled nightcap, shirt and bedclothes. Very clean and neat too was the bedroom opening on to the little front yard, beneath each window of the one-storeyed dwelling being a brilliant border of asters. The housewife also was a picture of tidiness, her cotton gown carefully patched and scrupulously clean. This worthy couple are said to be worth fifty thousand francs. The wife, a sexagenarian, does all the work of the house besides waiting on her good man, to whom she is devoted, but a married son and daughter-in-law share her duties at night. Here was no touch of sordidness or suggestion of "La Terre," instead a delightful picture of rustic dignity and ease. The housewife sold us half a bushel of pears, these two like their neighbours living by the produce of their small farm and garden.

I often dropped in upon Madame B—— to whom even morning calls were acceptable.

On the occasion of my farewell visit she had something pretty to say about one of my own novels, a French translation of which I had presented her.

"I suppose," I said, "that you have some books of your own?"

"Here they are," she said, depositing an armful on the table. "But I have never read much, and mostly *bibelots*" (trifles.)

Her poor little library consisted of *bibelots* indeed, a history of Jeanne d'Arc for children, and half a dozen other works, mostly school prizes of the kind awarded before school prizes in France were worth the paper on which they were printed.

CHAPTER VI
LARCHANT

There is a certain stimulating quality of elasticity and crispness in the French atmosphere which our own does not possess. France, moreover, with its seven climates—for the description of these, see Reclus' Geography—does undoubtedly offer longer, less broken, spells of hot summer weather than the United Kingdom. But let me for once and for all dispel a widespread illusion. The late Lord Lytton, when Ambassador in Paris, used to say that in the French capital you could procure any climate you pleased. And experience proves that without budging an inch you may in France get as many and as rapid climatic changes as anywhere else under the sun. At noon in mid-May last I was breakfasting with friends on the Champs Elysées, when my hostess put a match to the fire and my host jumped up and lighted six wax candles. So dense had become the heavens that we could no longer see to handle knives and forks! Hail, wind, darkness and temperature recalled a November squall at home. Yet the day before I had enjoyed perfect summer weather in the Jardin d'Acclimation. Invariableness is no more an attribute of the French climate than our own. Wherever we go we must take a change of dress, for all the world as if we were bound for the other side of the Tweed.

My first Sunday at Bourron, on this third visit, was of perfect stillness, unclouded brilliance and southern languor, heralding, so we fondly imagined, the very morrow for an excursion.

In the night a strong wind rose up, but as we had ordered a carriage for Larchant, and as carriages in these parts are not always to be had, as, moreover, grown folks no more than children like to defer their pleasure, off we set, two of the party on cycles forming a body guard. There seemed no likelihood of rain and in the forest we should not feel the wind.

For the first mile or two all went well. Far ahead of us our cyclists bowled gaily along in the forest avenues, all of us being sheltered from the wind. It was not till we skirted a wide opening that we felt the full force of the tornado, soon overtaking our blowzed, dishevelled companions, both on foot and looking miserable enough.

We re-entered the forest, and a little later, emerging from the fragrant depths of a pine wood, got our first view of Larchant, coming suddenly upon what looks like a cathedral towering above the plain, at its base a clustering village, whitewashed brown-roofed houses amid vineyards and orchards.

{Illustration}

A grandiose view it is, recalling the minaret of Mansourah near Tclemcen in Algeria, that gigantic monolith apparently carved out of Indian gold and cleft in two like a pomegranate.

Slowly we wound up towards the village, the wind, or rather hurricane, gathering in force as we went. It was indeed no easy task to get a nearer view of the church; more than once we were compelled to beat a retreat, whilst it seemed really unsafe to linger underneath such a ruin.

Imagine the tower of St. Jacques in the Rue de Rivoli split in two, the upright half standing in a bare wind-swept level, and you have some faint notion of Larchant. On nearer approach such an impression of grandeur is by no means diminished. This magnificent parish church, in part a ruin, in part restored, rather grows upon one upon closer inspection. Reparation, for want of funds, has stopped short at the absolutely necessary. The body of the church has been so far restored as to be fit for use, but its crowning glory, the tower, remains a torso.

The front view suggests no such dilapidation. How long will the shell of that lofty twelfth century tower remain standing? To my mind it hangs over the low, one-storeyed houses at its feet, a veritable sword of Damocles, sooner or later sure to fall with crushing force. The porch shows much beautiful carving, unfortunately defaced, and the interior some perfect specimens of pure Gothic arches, the whole whitewashed and bare as a barn.

Larchant in the middle ages was a famous pilgrimage, and in the days of Charles IX. a halting stage on the road to Italy. It does not seem to attract many English pilgrims at the present time. Anyhow tea-making here seems a wholly unknown art. In a fairly clean inn, however, a good-natured landlady allowed us to make ourselves at home alike in kitchen and pantry. One of our party unearthed a time-honoured tea-pot—we had of course taken the precaution of carrying tea with us—one by one milk and sugar were forthcoming in what may be called wholesale fashion, milk-jugs and sugar-basins being apparently articles of superfluity, and in company of a charming old dog and irresistible kitten, also of some quiet wayfarers, we five-o'clocked merrily enough.

Our business at Larchant was not wholly archaeological. Buffeted as we were by the hurricane, we managed to pay a visit in search of eggs and poultry for the table at home.

If peasant and farming life in France certainly from time to time reminds us of Zola's "La Terre," we are also reminded of an aspect which the great novelist ignores. As will be seen from the following sketch sordidness and aspiration oft times, I am almost tempted to say, and most often, go hand in hand.

We see one generation addicted to an existence so laborious and material as to have no counterpart in England; under the same roof growing up another, sharing all the advantages of social and intellectual progress.

Not far from the church we called upon a family of large and wealthy farmers, owners of the soil they cultivate, millionaires by comparison with our neighbours at Bourron.

We arrived in the midst of a busy time, a steam corn thresher plying in the vast farm-yard. The interior of the big, straggling farm-house we did not see, but two aged women dressed like poor peasants received us in the kitchen, a dingy, unswept, uninviting place, as are most farm-house kitchens in France. These old ladies were respectively mother-in-law and aunt of the farmer, whose wife, the real mistress of the house, soon came in. This tall, stout, florid, brawny-armed woman was evidently what French folks call *une maîtresse femme*, a first-rate housewife and manager; a somewhat awe-inspiring person she looked as she stood before us, arms akimbo, her short coarse serge skirt showing shoes well acquainted with stable and neat-house, one dirty blue cotton apron worn over another equally dirty. Now, my hostess, as I have said, wanted to purchase some poultry for the table, and here comes in the moral of my story. Vainly the lady begged and begged again for a couple of chickens. "But we want them for our Parisians," the three farming women reiterated, one echoing the other. "Our Parisians, our Parisians," the words were repeated a dozen times. And as was explained to me afterwards, "our Parisians," for whom the pick of the poultry yard was being reserved, were the two sons of the rather forbidding-looking matron before us, young gentlemen being educated in a Paris Lycée, and both of them destined for the learned professions!

This side of rural life, this ambition, akin to what we see taking quite another form among ourselves, Zola does not sufficiently realize. Shocking indeed were the miserliness and materialism of such existences but for the element of self-denial, this looking ahead for those to follow after. How differently, for instance, the farm-house and its group must have appeared, but for the evident pride and hopes centred in *nos Parisiens*, who knows?—perhaps youths destined to attain the first rank in official or political callings!

The farther door of the smoke-dried kitchen opened on to the farm-yard, around which were stables and neat-houses. In the latter the mistress of the house proudly drew our attention to a beautiful blue cow, grey in our ignorance we had called it, one of a score or more of superb kine all now reclining on their haunches before being turned out to pasture. In front, cocks and hens disported themselves on a dunghill, whilst beyond, the steam corn thresher was at work, every hand being called into requisition. No need here for particulars and figures. The superabundant wealth, so carefully husbanded for the two youths in Paris, was self-evident.

The tornado, with threatening showers and the sight of a huge tree just uprooted by the road side, necessitated the shortest possible cut home. In fair weather a prolongation of our drive would have given us a sight of some famous rocks of this rocky forest. But we carried home memories enough for one day.

CHAPTER VII
RECLOSES.

This ancient village, reached by the forest, is one of the most picturesque of the many picturesque places hereabouts. Quitting a stretch of pinewood we traverse flat cultivated land, gradually winding up towards a long straggling village surmounted by a lofty church tower of grey stone. On either side of this street are enclosed farm-houses, the interiors being as pictorial as can be imagined. Untidy as are most French homesteads, for peasant farmers pay little court to the Graces, there is always a bit of flower garden. Sometimes this flower garden is aerial, a bower of roses on the roof sometimes amid the incongruous surroundings of pig styes or manure heaps. This region is a petunia land; wherever we go we find a veritable blaze of petunia blossoms, pale mauve, deepest rose, purple and white massed together without order or view to effect. In one of the little fortresses—for so these antique farmhouses may be called—we saw a rustic piazza, pillars and roof of rude unhewn stone blazing with petunias, no attempt whatever at making the structure whole, symmetrical or graceful to the eye. It seems as if these homely though rich farmers, or rather farmers' wives, could not do without flowers, above the street jutting many aerial gardens, the only touch of beauty in the work-a-day picture. These interiors would supply artists with the most captivating subjects. The women, their skins brown and wrinkled as ripe, shelled walnuts, their head-dress a blue and white kerchief neatly folded and knotted, the expression of their faces shrewd and kindly, all contribute to the charm of the scene.

Here as elsewhere the young women and girls affect a little fashion and finery on Sundays.

We should not know unless we were told that Recloses was one of the richest villages in these parts. On this Sunday, September 1st, 1901, in one place a steam thresher was at work, although for the most part folks seemed to be taking their ease in their holiday garb. Perhaps the difficulty of procuring the machine accounted for the fact of seeing it on a Sunday.

One of the farm-yards showed a charming menagerie of poultry and the prettiest rabbits in the world, all disporting themselves in most amicable fashion. Here, as elsewhere, when we stopped to admire, the housewife came out, pleased to interchange a few words with us. The sight of Recloses is not, however, its long line of little walled-in farm-houses, but the curious rocky platform at the end of the village, perforated with holes always full of water, and the stupendous view thence obtained—an ocean of sombre green unrelieved by a single sail.

Already the vast panorama of forest shows signs of autumn, light touches of yellow relieving the depths of solemn green. On such a day of varied cloudland the perspective must be quite different, and perhaps even more beautiful than under a burning cloudless sky, no soft gradations between the greens and the blues. The little pools or perforations breaking the surface of the broad platform, acres of rocks, are, I believe, unexplained phenomena. In the driest season these openings contain water, presumably forced upwards from hidden springs. The pools, just now covered with green slime, curiously spot the grey surface of the rocks.

If, leaving the world of forest to our right, we continue our journey in the direction of Chapelle la Reine, we overlook a vast plain the population of which is very different from that of the smiling fertile prosperous valley of the Loing. This plain, extending to Étampes and Pithiviers, might, I am told, possibly have suggested to Zola some scenes and characters of "La Terre." A French friend of mine, well acquainted with these parts, tells me that at any rate there, if anywhere, the great novelist might have found suggestions for such a work. The soil is arid, the cultivation is primitive in the extreme and the people are rough and uncouth. The other day an English resident at Marlotte, when cycling among these villages of the plain inquired his way of a countryman.

"You are not a Frenchman?" quoth the latter before giving the desired information.

"No I am not" was the reply.

"You are not an American?"

"No, I am an Englishman."

"Ah!" was the answer, "I smelt you out sure enough" (*Je vous ai bien senti*). Whereupon he proceeded to put the wayfarer on his right road.

As a rule French peasants are exceedingly courteous to strangers, but these good people of the plain seldom come in contact with the tourist world, their country not being sufficiently picturesque even to attract the cyclist.

The curious thirteenth-century church of Recloses had long been an art pilgrimage. It contains, or at least should contain, some of the most wonderful wood carvings in France; figures and groups of figures highly realistic in the best sense of the word. These sculptures, unfortunately, we were not able to inspect a second time; exhibited in the Paris Exhibition they had not yet been replaced.

It is a beautiful drive from Recloses to Bourron by the Croix de Saint Hérem. A little way out of the village we came upon a pretty scene, people, in family groups, playing croquet under the trees. Dancing also goes on in summer as in the olden time. It was curious as we drove along to note the behaviour of my friend's dog: it never for a moment closed its eyes, and yet there was nothing to look at but avenue after avenue of trees. What could the little animal find so fascinating in the somewhat monotonous sight? A friend at home assures me that a pet of her own enjoyed drives from purely snobbish motives; his great gratification arising from the sense of superiority over fellow dogs compelled to trudge on foot. But in these woodland solitudes there was no room for such a sentiment, not a dog being visible, only now and then a cyclist flashing by.

There is no more splendid cycling ground in the world than this forest of Fontainebleau.

Shakespeare says:—

> *"This guest of summer,*
> *The temple-haunting martlet, does approve*
> *By his loved mansionry that the heaven's breath*
> *Smells wooingly here: no jutty frieze, buttress,*
> *Nor coigne of vantage, but this bird hath made*

> *His pendent bed, and procreant cradle: Where they*
> *Most breed and haunt, I have observed the air*
> *Is delicate."*

About this time at Bourron the village street was alive with swallows preparing, I presume, for departure southwards. A beautiful sight it was to see these winged congregations evidently concerting their future movements.

Another feature to be mentioned is the number of large handsome moths frequenting these regions. One beautiful creature as large as a swallow used to fly into our dining room every evening for warmth; fastening itself to the wall it would there remain undisturbed until the morning.

I finish these reminiscences of Bourron by the following citation from Balzac's "Ursule Mirouët":—

"On entering Nemours at five o'clock in the morning, Ursule woke up feeling quite ashamed of her untidiness, and of encountering Savinien's look of admiration. During the time that the diligence took to come from Bouron (*sic*), where it stopped a few minutes, the young man had observed Ursule. He had noted the candour of her mind, the beauty of her person, the whiteness of her complexion, the delicacy of her features, the charm of the voice which had uttered the short and expressive sentence, in which the poor child said everything, while wishing to say nothing. In short I do not know what presentiment made him see in Ursule the woman whom the doctor had depicted, framed in gold, with these magic words:—'Seven to eight hundred thousand francs!'"

Holiday tourists in these parts cannot do better than put this love-story in their pockets.

CHAPTER VIII
NEMOURS.

"Who knows Nemours," wrote Balzac, "knows that nature there is as beautiful as art," and again he dwells upon the charm of the sleepy little town memorialized in "Ursule Mirouët."

The delicious valley of Loing indeed fascinated Balzac almost as much as his beloved Touraine.

As his recently published letters to Madame Hanska have shown us, several of his greatest novels were written in this neighbourhood, whilst in the one named above we have a setting as striking as that of "Eugenie Grandet" or "Béatrix." A ten minutes' railway journey brings us to Nemours, one of the few French towns, by the way, in which Arthur Young lost his temper. Here is his own account of the incident:—

"Sleep at Nemours, where we met with an innkeeper who exceeded in knavery all we had met with, either in France or Italy: for supper, we had a *soupe maigre*, a partridge and a chicken roasted, a plate of celery, a small cauliflower, two bottles of poor *vin du Pays*, and a dessert of two biscuits and four apples: here is the bill:—Potage 1 liv. 10f.—Perdrix 2 liv. 10f.—Poulet 2 liv.—Céleri 1 liv. 4f.—Choufleur 2 liv.—Pain et dessert 2 liv.—Feu et appartement 6 liv.—Total 19 liv. 8f. Against so impudent an extortion we remonstrated severely but in vain. We then insisted on his signing the bill, which, after many evasions, he did, *à l'étoile, Foulliare*. But having been carried to the inn, not as the star, but the *écu de France*, we suspected some deceit: and going out to examine the premises, we found the sign to be really the *écu*, and learned on enquiry that his own name was Roux, instead of *Foulliare*: he was not prepared for this detection, or for the execration we poured on such infamous conduct; but he ran away in an instant and hid himself till we were gone. In justice to the world, however, such a fellow ought to be marked out."

I confess I do not myself find such charges excessive. From a very different motive, Nemours put me as much out of temper as it had done my great predecessor a hundred years before. Will it be believed that a town memorialized by the great, perhaps *the* greatest, French novelist, could not produce its title of honour, in other words a copy of "Ursule Mirouët"?

This town of 4,000 and odd souls and chef-lieu of department does not possess a bookseller's shop. We did indeed see in a stationer's window one or two penny books, among these an abridged translation of "Uncle Tom's Cabin." But a friendly wine merchant, who seemed to take my reproaches very much to heart, assured us that in the municipal library all Balzac's works were to be found, besides many valuable books dealing with local history.

Cold comfort this for tourists who want to buy a copy of the Nemours story! As we stroll about the grass-grown streets, we feel that railways, telephones and the rest have very little changed Nemours since Balzac's descriptions, written three-quarters of a century ago.

The sweet and pastoral surroundings of the place are in strong contrast with the sordid next-of-kin peopling the pages of his romance. Beyond the fine old church of rich grey stone, you obtain as enchanting a view as the valley of the Loing can show, a broad, crystal-clear river winding amid picturesque architecture, richest and most varied foliage, ash and weeping willow mingling with deeper-hued beech and alder. It is difficult, almost impossible, to describe the charm of this riverside scenery. In one passage of his novel, Balzac compares the view to the scenery of an opera, and in very truth every feature forms a whole so harmonious as to suggest artistic arrangement.

Nature and accident have effected the happiest possible combination of wood, water and building stone. Nothing is here to mar the complete picture. Grandly the cathedral-like church and fine old château stand out to-day against the brilliant sky, soft grey stone and dark brown making subdued harmonies. Formerly Nemours was surrounded by woods, hence its name. People are said to attain here a very great age, life being tranquil and the nature of the people somewhat lethargic.

Amongst the more energetic inhabitants are a lady dentist and her sister, who between them do a first rate business.

French peasants never dream of indulging in false teeth; such an idea would never enter the head of even the richest. But an aching tooth interferes with the labours of the farm, and must be got rid of at any cost. This young lady *chirurgien et dentiste*, such is the name figuring on her door plate, is not only most expert in using the forceps, but is attractive and pretty.

Her charges are two francs for a visit or operation; in partnership with her is a sister who does the accounts, and as nuns and sisters of charity unprovided with certificates are no longer allowed to draw teeth, act as midwives and cut off limbs, country doctors and dentists of either sex have now a fair chance.

No town in this part of France suffered more during the German invasion. The municipal authorities had at first decided upon making a bold stand, thus endeavouring to check the enemy's advance on Paris. Differences of opinion arose, prudential counsels prevailed, and it was through a mistaken order that a Prussian detachment was attacked near the town. The consequences were appalling. The station was burned to the ground, enormous contributions in money and material were exacted from the town, some of the authorities were made to travel on the railways with the invaders, and others were carried off to remote fortresses of Brandenburg and there kept as prisoners for nine months.

The account of all these incidents, written by a victim, may be consulted in a volume of the town library.

If people frequently attain the age of a hundred in Nemours, as I was assured, it is rather due to placid temperament than to intellectual torpor. The town possesses learned societies, and a member of its archaeological association has published a book of great local interest and value, viz:—"Nemours, Temps Géologiques, Temps Préhistoriques, Temps Historiques, par E. Doigneau, Membre de la Société Archéologique de Seine-et-Marne, Ancien Vice Président de la section de Fontainebleau, Paris."

Strange to say, although this neighbourhood has offered a rich field for prehistoric research, Nemours as yet possesses no museum, I do verily believe the first French town of any size I have ever found in France without one at least in embryo. For the cyclist the run from Bourron to Nemours is delightful, on the hottest day in the year spinning along broad well-wooded roads, with lovely perspectives from time to time.

CHAPTER IX
LA CHARITÉ-SUR-LOIRE.

From Bourron, in September, 1900, I journeyed with a friend to La Charité, a little town four hours off.

It is ever with feelings of pleasurable anticipation that I approach any French town for the first time. The number of these, alas! now being few, I have of late years been compelled to restrain curiosity, leaving one or two dreamed-of spots for the future, saying with Wordsworth:—

> "Should life be dull and spirits low,
>
> 'Twill soothe us in our sorrow,
>
> That earth has something yet to show,
>
> The bonny holms of Yarrow."

La Charité, picturesque of the picturesque—according to French accounts, English, we have none—for many years had been a Yarrow to me, a reserve of delight, held back from sheer Epicureanism.

As, on the 12th of September, the cumbersome old omnibus rattled over the unpaved streets, both to myself and fellow traveller came a feeling of disenchantment. We had apparently reached one more of those sleepy little *chefs-lieux* familiar to both, places of interest certainly, the sleepiest having some architectural gem or artistic treasure. But here was surely no Yarrow!

A few minutes later we discovered our error. Hardly had we reached our rooms in the more than old-fashioned Hôtel du Grand Monarque, than from a side window, we caught sight of the Loire; so near, indeed, lay the bright, blue river, that we could almost have thrown pebbles into its clear depths; quitting the hotel, half a dozen steps, no more were needed, an enchanting scene burst upon the view.

Most beautiful is the site of La Charité, built terrace-wise, not on the skirts but on the very hem of the Loire, here no revolutionary torrent, sweeping away whole villages, leaving only church steeples visible above the engulfing waters, as I had once seen it at Nantes, but a broad, smooth, crystal expanse of sky-blue. Over against the handsome stone bridge to-day having its double in the limpid water, we see a little islanded hamlet crowned with picturesque church tower; and, placing ourselves midway between the town and its suburban twin, obtain vast and lovely perspectives. Westward, gradually purpling as evening wears on, rises the magnificent height of Sancerre, below, amid low banks bordered with poplar, flowing the Loire. Eastward, looking towards Nevers, our eyes rest on the same broad sheet of blue; before us, straight as an arrow, stretches the French road of a pattern we know so well, an apparently interminable avenue of plane or poplar trees. The river is low at this season, and the velvety brown sands recall the sea-shore when the tide is out. Exquisite, at such an hour are the reflections, every object having its mirrored self in the transparent waves, the lights and shadows of twilight making lovely effects.

As is the case with Venice, La Charité should be reached by river, and a pity it seems that little steamers do not ply between all the principal towns on the Loire. How enchanting, like the immortal Vert-Vert, of Gresset's poem, to travel from Nevers to the river's mouth!

If I had headed this paper merely with the words "La Charité," I should surely be supposed to treat of some charitable institution in France, or of charity as worked out in the abstract, for this first of Christian virtues has given the place its name, presumably perpetuating the charitableness of its abbatial founders. Just upon two thousand years ago, some pious monks of the order of Cluny settled here, calling their foundation La Charité. Gradually a town grew around the abbey walls, and what better name for any than this? So La Charité it was in early feudal times, and La Charité it remains in our own.

The place itself is as antiquated and behindhand as any I have seen in France, which is saying a good deal. A French gentleman, native of these parts, told me that in his grandfather's time our Hôtel du Grand Monarque enjoyed a fine reputation. In many respects it deserves the same still, excellent beds, good cooking, quietude and low prices not being so common as they might be in French provincial inns. The house, too, is curious, what with its spiral stone staircases, little passages leading to one room here, to another there—as if in former days travellers objected to walls that adjoined those of other people—and unaccountable levels, it is impossible to understand whether you were on the first floor or the second floor, house-top, or basement. Our bedrooms, for instance, reached by one of the spiral stone staircases just named never used by myself without apprehension, landed us on the edge of a poultry yard; I suppose a wide bit of roof had been converted into this use, but it was quite impossible to make out any architectural plan. These rooms adjoining this *basse-cour*, hens and chicks would enter unceremoniously and pick up the crumbs we threw to them. Fastidious tourists might resent so primitive a state of things, the hotel, I should say, remaining exactly what it was under the Ancien Régime. The beauty and interest of various kinds around, more than make up for small drawbacks. Here the archaeologist will not grudge several days. Ruined as it is, the ancient abbey may be reconstructed in the mind's eye by the help of what we see before us. The fragments of crumbling wall, the noble tower and portal, the delicately sculptured pillars, cornices, and arches, enable us to build up the whole, just as Cuvier made out an entire skeleton from the examination of a single bone. These grand architectural fragments have not been neglected by the learned. Unfortunately, and exceptionally, La Charité possesses neither public library nor museum, but at Nevers the traveller would surely find a copy of Prosper Merimée's "Notes Archéologiques" in which is a minute account of these.

Alike without and within the ruins show a medley of styles and richest ornamentation.

{Illustration}

The superb north-west tower, that forms so striking an object from the river, is said to be in the Burgundian style; rather should we put it after a Burgundian style, so varied and heterogeneous are the churches coming under this category. Again, the guide books inform us that the open space between this tower and the church was occupied by the narthex, a vast outer portico of ancient Burgundian churches used for the reception of penitents, catechumens, and strangers. All interested in ecclesiastical architecture should visit the abbey church of Vézelay, which possesses a magnificent narthex of two storeys, restored by the late Viollet le Duc. Vézelay, by the way, may be easily reached from La Charité.

Next to the elaborate sculptures of this grand tower, will be noted the superb colour of the building stone, carved out of deep-hued gold it looks under the burning blue sky. And of a piece are arch, portico and column, one and all helping us to reconstruct the once mighty abbey, home of a brotherhood so powerful as to necessitate disciplinary measures on the part of the Pope.

The interior of the church shows the same elaborateness of detail, and the same mixture of styles, the Romanesque-Burgundian predominating, so, at least, affirm authorities.

The idler and lover of the picturesque will not find time hang heavy on his hands here. Very sweet are the riverside views, no matter on which side we obtain them, and the quaintest little staircases of streets run from base to summit of the pyramidally-built town. A climb of a quarter of an hour takes us to an admirable coign of vantage just above the abbey church, and commanding a view of Sancerre and the river. That little town, so splendidly placed, is celebrated for its eight months' defence as a Huguenot stronghold.

La Charité, with most mediaeval towns, was fortified, one old city gate still remaining.

To-day, as when that charming writer, Émile Montégut visited the place more than a generation ago, the townspeople ply their crafts and domestic callings abroad. In fine weather, no work that can possibly be done in the open air is done within four walls. Another curious feature of these engaging old streets, is the number of blacksmiths' shops. It would seem as if all the horses, mules, and donkeys of the Nièvre were brought hither to be shod, the smithy fires keeping up a perpetual illumination.

A third and still more noteworthy point is the infrequency—absence, I am inclined to say—of cabarets. Soberest of the sober, orderliest of the orderly, appear these good folks of La Charité, les Caritates as they are called, nor, apparently, has tradition demoralised them. One might expect that a town dedicated to the virtue of almsgiving would abound in beggars. Not one did we see.

CHAPTER X
POUGUES.

If an ugly name could kill a place, Pougues must surely have been ruined as a health resort centuries ago. Coming, too, after that soothing, harmoniously named La Charité, could any configuration of letters grate more harshly on the ear? Truth to tell, my travelling companion and myself had a friendly little altercation about Pougues. It seemed impossible to believe pleasant things of a town so labelled. But the reputation of Pougues dates from Hercules and Julius Caesar, both heroes, it is said, having had recourse to its mineral springs! Coming from legend to history, we find that Pougues, or, at least, the waters of Pougues, were patronised by the least objectionable son of Catherine de Medicis, Henri II. of France and runaway King of Poland. Imputing his disorders to sorcery, he was thus reassured by a sensible physician named Pidoux: "Sire, the malady from which you suffer is due to no witchcraft. Lead a quiet life for ten weeks, and drink the water of Pougues." The best king France ever had, namely, the gay Gascon, and after him Louis XIII., by no means one of the worst, had recourse to Pougues waters; also that arch-voluptuary and arch-despot, the Sun-King, who imagined that even syntax and prosody must bow to his will. {Footnote: One day the young king ordered his carriage, saying, "*mon* carrosse," instead of "*ma* carrosse," the French word being derived from the Italian feminine, *carrozza*. On being gently corrected, the king flew into a passion, declaring that masculine he had called it, and masculine it should remain, which it has done to this day, so the story runs. Let the Republic look to it!} And Madame de Sevigné—for whom, however, I have scant love, for did she not hail the revocation of the Edict of Nantes?—Madame de Sevigné honoured Pougues with an epigram.

A second Purgatory she styled the douches, and, doubtless, in those non-washing days, a second Purgatory it would have been to most folks.

To Pougues, nevertheless, we went, and if these notes induce the more enterprising of my countrypeople to do the same next summer, they are not likely to repent of the experiment. Never, indeed, was a little Eden of coolness, freshness, and greenery more abominably used by its sponsors, whilst the name of so many French townlings are a poem in themselves!

From a view of sky blue waters and smooth brown sands we were transported to a world of emerald green verdure and richest foliage, interpenetrated with golden light. On this 14th of September the warmth and dazzlingness of mid-summer still reigned at Pougues; and the scenery in which we suddenly found ourselves, bosquets, dells, and glades, with all the charm but without the savageness of the forest, recalled the loveliest lines of the laziest poet:—

> *"Was naught around but images of rest,*
>
> *And flowery beds, that slumberous influence kest{1},*
>
> *Sleep-soothing groves and quiet lawns between,*
>
> *From poppies breathed; and beds of pleasant green."*

{Footnote 1: Cast}

A drive of a few minutes had landed us in the heart of this little Paradise, baths and Casino standing in the midst of park-like grounds. Apparently Pougues, that is to say, the Pougues-les-Eaux of later days, has been cut out of natural woodland, the Casino gardens and its surroundings being rich in forest trees of superb growth and great variety. The wealth of foliage gives this new fashionable little watering-place an enticingly rural appearance, nor is the attraction of water wholly wanting. To quote once more a most quotable, if little read, poet:—

> *"Meantime, unnumbered glittering streamlets played,*
>
> *And hurled everywhere their water's sheen,*
>
> *That, as they bickered through the sunny glade,*
>
> *Though restless still, themselves a lulling murmur made."*

A pretty little lake, animated with swans, varies the woodland scenery, and tropical birds in an aviary lend brilliant bits of colour. The usual accessories of a health resort are, of course, here—reading room, concert hall, theatre, and other attractions, rapidly turning the place into a lesser Vichy. The number and magnificence of the hotels, the villas and *cottages*, that have sprung up on every side, bespeak the popularity of Pougues-les-Eaux, as it is now styled, the surname adding more dignity than harmoniousness. One advantage Pougues possesses over its rivals, is position. At Aix-les-Bains, Plombières, Salins, and how many other inland spas, you are literally wedged in between shelving hills. If you want to enjoy wide horizons, and anything like a breeze, you must get well outside the town. Never in hot, dusty, crowded cities have I felt so half-suffocated as at the two first named places. Pougues, on the contrary, lies in a broad expanse of beautifully varied woodland and champaign, no more appropriate site conceivable for the now popular air-cure. "Pougues-les-Eaux, Cure d'Eau and Cure d'Air," is now its proud title, folks flocking hither, not only to imbibe its delicious, ice-cold, sparkling waters, but to drink in its highly nourishing air. The iron-gaseous waters resemble in properties those of Spa and Vichy. From one to five tumblers are ordered a day, according to the condition of the drinker, a little stroll between each dose being advisable. With regard to the air-cure, visitors are reminded that at Pougues they find the four kinds of walking exercise recommended by a German specialist, namely, that on quite level ground; secondly, a very gradual climb; thirdly, a somewhat steeper bit of up-hill; and, fourthly, the really arduous ascent of Mont Givre. In order to entice health-seekers, all kinds of gratifications await them on the summit, restaurant, dairy, reading room, tennis court, and croquet ground, to say nothing of a panorama almost unrivalled in eastern France. We have, indeed, climbed the Eiffel Tower, in other words, are on a level with that final stage from which floats the Tricolour. Looking east we behold the sombre Morvan and Nevers rising above the Loire, whilst westward, beyond the plain and the Loire, may be descried the cathedral of Bourges. How many regions visited and revisited by myself now lie before my eyes as on a map—the Berri, Georges Sand's country, the little Celtic kingdom of the Morvan, on the borders of which, for so many years, that charming writer, Philip Gilbert Hamerton, made his home; the Nivernais, with its souvenirs of Vert-Vert and Mazarin, or, rather, Mazarin and Vert-Vert, the Department of the Allier made from the ancient province of the Bourbonnais.

A wanderer in France should never be without his Arthur Young. That "wise and honest traveller," of course, had been before us, but travelling in a contrary direction. "From the hill that descends to Pougues," he wrote on his way from Nevers to Fontainebleau, in 1790, "is an extensive view to the north, and after Pouilly a (*sic*) fine scenery, with the Loire doubling through it." But the great farmer made this journey in mid-winter, thus missing its charm. And Arthur Young was ever too intent upon crops and roots to notice wild flowers. Had he traversed this region earlier in the year, he might have missed an exquisite feature, namely, the sweeps of autumn crocus. Just now the rich pastures around Pougues, as well as suburban lawns and wayside spaces, were tinted with delicate mauve, the ground being literally carpeted with these flowers. It was as if the lightest possible veil of pale purple covered the turf, the same profusion being visible on every side.

One final word about this sweet and most unmusically named place. On no occasion and nowhere have I been received with more cordiality than at dear little Pougues, a place I was told there utterly ignored by my country people. I do honestly believe, indeed, that myself and fellow traveller were the first English folk to wander about those delicious gardens, and taste the incomparable waters, cool, sparkling, invigorating as those of Spa.

One enterprising proprietor of an excellent hotel was so anxious to secure an English *clientèle*, the best *clientèle* in the world, so hotel keepers aver, that she offered me a handsome percentage on any visitors I would send her. In the most delicate manner I could command, I gave her to understand that my inquiries about Pougues were not made from a business point of view, but that I should certainly proclaim its many attractions on the house-tops.

CHAPTER XI
NEVERS AND MOULINS.

I found the well-remembered Hôtel de France much as I had left it, just upon twenty years before, every whit as quiet, comfortable, and moderate in price, indeed, one of the best provincial hotels of France. The dear old woman then employed as waitress, had, of course, long since gone to her rest, and the landlord and landlady were new to me. But, the traditions of an excellent house were evidently kept up, accommodation, meanwhile, having been greatly enlarged.

A place is like a book; if worth knowing at all, to be returned to again and again. After the first brief visit so many years ago, I wrote, "I envy the traveller who for the first time stands on the bridge of Nevers." And more imposing, more exhilarating still, seemed the view from the same spot now; under the brilliant sky, in the clear atmosphere, every feature standing out as in a mosaic proudly dominating all, the Cathedral, with its mass of sombre architecture; stretching wide to right and left, the gay, prosperous-looking city; white villas rising one above the other, hanging gardens and terraced lawns, making greenery and verdure in mid-air. On the occasion of my first visit in August, 1881, the Loire was so low as to appear a mere thread of palest blue amid white sands; at the time I now write of, broad and beautiful it flowed beneath the noble bridge, a deep twilight sky reflected in its limpid waters.

How well I remember the first sight of this scene years ago! Then it was early morning of market day, and, pouring in from the country, I had met crowds of peasants with their products, the men in blue blouses, the women in neat white coiffes, some bearing huge baskets on their heads, others drawing heavily laden barrows, driving donkey-carts, the piled-up fruit and vegetables making a blaze of colour. For three sous I recorded the purchase of more wild strawberries, peaches, and greengages than I knew what to do with, each grower doing business on his own account, no middleman to share his profits; choicest fruit and vegetables to be had almost for the asking. On this lovely Sunday evening plenty of peasant folk were about, the men fishing in the Loire, the women minding their children under the trees. But I noted here, as elsewhere, a gradual disappearance of the blue blouse and white coiffe. Broadcloth and bonnets are fast superseding the homely, picturesque dress of former days.

The aerial residences just mentioned are characteristic of riverside Nevers. Craning our necks as we strolled to and fro, we remarked how much life in such altitudes must resemble that of a balloon, folks being thus lifted above the hubbub, malodours, and microbes of the human bee-hive below. For my own part I prefer a turnpike level, despite the engaging aspect of those rose-girt verandahs, bowers, and lawns on a level with the cathedral tower.

"Nevers makes a fine appearance, rising proudly from the Loire," wrote Arthur Young, "but on the first entrance it is like a thousand other places."

But the indefatigable apostle of the turnip had no time for archaeology on his great tour, or he would have discovered that Nevers possesses more than one architectural gem of the first water. The cathedral certainly, alike without and within, must take rank after those of Chartres, Le Mans, Reims, and how many others! but the exquisite little church of St. Étienne and the Ducal Palace, are both perfect in their way, and will enchant all lovers of harmony and proportion. The first, another specimen of so-called Romanesque-Burgundian, has to be looked for, standing as it does in a kind of *cul de sac*; the second occupies a conspicuous site, forms, indeed, the centre-piece and crowning ornament of the town. Daintiest of the dainty, this fairy-like Italian palace in the heart of France, reminds us that once upon a time Nevers was the seat of Italian dukes, the last of whom was a nephew of Mazarin. The great Cardinal, "whose heart was more French than his speech," and who served France so well, despite his nationality and his nepotism, having purchased the Nivernais of a Gonzague, finally incorporated it into the French crown in 1659.

To this day, Nevers remains true to its Italian traditions. Go into the tiniest suburban street, enter the poorest little general shop, and you are reminded of the art that made the city famous hundreds of years ago, an art introduced by a Duke of Mantua, relation of Catherine de Medicis. It was in the sixteenth century, that this feudal lord of the Nivernais summoned Italian potters hither, among these a native of Faenza. Under his direction a manufactory of faïence was established, the ware resembling that of his native city, scriptural and allegorical subjects traced in manganese. The unrivalled blue glaze of Nevers is of later date. Just as Rouen potters were celebrated for their reds, the Nivernais surpassed them in blues. No French or foreign potters ever achieved an azure of equal depth and purity.

The golden age of Nevers majolica belongs to that early period, but the highly ornamented faïence now produced in its ateliers, shows taste and finish, and in the town itself may be found charming things as cheap as, if not cheaper than, our commonest earthenware.

As I write, I have before me some purchases made at a small general dealer's, a plate, and two small amphora-shaped vases, costing a few sous each. The colouring of this cheap pottery is very harmonious, and the glaze remarkable for its brilliance. The shopwoman, with whom we had a pleasant chat, did not seem astonished at our admiration for her goods.

"I sell lots of such things as you have just bought, to folks like you" *(de votre genre)*, she said, "strangers who like to carry away a souvenir of the place, and all my ware comes from the same manufacture."

To-day Nevers thrives upon ornamental majolica. A hundred and ten years ago it throve upon plates and dishes commemorating the Revolution. In the upper storey of the Ducal Palace we may read revolutionary annals in faïence, every event being memorialised by a piece of porcelain.

Curious enough is this record in earthenware, one stormy day after another being thus commemorated; and perhaps more curious still is the evident care with which these fragile objects have been preserved. Throughout the Napoleonic era they might pass—had not gold pieces then on one side the portrait of "Napoleon Empereur," on the obverse "République Français"?—but when Louis XVIII was brought back by his foreign friends, how was it that there came no general smashing, a great flinging of revolutionary potsherds to the dunghill? Safe enough now is the Nivernais collection, under the roof of the Ducal Palace, the rude designs and commonness of the ware strikingly contrasted with the exquisite things around.

In close proximity to these cheap plates, dedicated to the Phrygian cap and sans-culottism, are the very choicest specimens of Nevers faïence of priceless value. Why the municipality, as a rule so generous towards the public, should thus inconveniently house its treasure, is inconceivable.

The museum is reached by a long spiral staircase, without banister or support, and a false step must certainly result in a broken leg, or, perhaps, neck! The room also contains a striking portrait of Theodore de Bèze, the great French reformer, who, then an aged man, penned a letter, sublime in its force and simplicity, to Henry IV., conjuring him not to abandon the Protestant faith. The mention of this fact recalls an interesting experience. I here allude to the incontestable advance of Protestantism in France. The traveller whose acquaintance with the country began a quarter of a century ago, cannot fail to be impressed with this fact. Alike in towns large and small, new places of worship have sprung up, Nevers now possessing an Evangelical church. And good was it to hear the appreciation of the little Protestant community from my Catholic landlady.

"Yes," she said, "the Protestants here are worthy of all respect (*dignes gens*) and the pastor also; I esteem him much." Evidently the Lemaitre-Coppée-Déroulède dictum, "Only the Catholic can be called a Frenchman," is not accepted at Nevers.

In dazzlingly brilliant weather, and amid glowing scenery, we continued our journey to Moulins, as we travelled by rail, and not by road unable to identify "the little opening in the road leading to a thicket" where Sterne discovered Maria. Has anyone ever identified the spot I wonder, poplar, small brook and the rest?

Too soon were we also for "the heyday of the vintage, when Nature is pouring her abundance into everyone's lap." For the vintage, indeed, one must go farther. Sterne must have been thinking of Burgundy when he penned that line, or the phylloxera has brought about a transformation, vineyards here being changed into pastures. The scenery of the Allier, like that around Autun, recalls many parts of England. Meadows set around with hedges; little rises of green hill here and there; cattle browsing by quiet streams; just such pictures as we may see in our own Midlands. I well remember a remark of the late Philip Gilbert Hamerton on this subject. We were strolling near his home, in the neighbourhood of Autun, one day, when he pointed to the landscape over against us.

"How like that is to many an English scene," he said; "and maybe it was the English aspect of this region that tempted me to settle here." I had paid Moulins a hasty visit many years before, but, unlike Nevers and so many French towns, the *chef-lieu* of the Allier does not improve upon further acquaintance. And I surmise, that such is the impression of my country people generally. English travellers must be few and far between at Moulins, or why should the appearance of two English ladies attract so much curiosity? Wherever we went, the good folks of Moulins, alike rich and poor, turned round to have a good look at us, even stopping short to stare. All this was done without any rudeness or remark, but such extraordinary behaviour can only be accounted for by the foregoing supposition. For some reason or other our compatriots do not, like Sterne and Maria go to Moulins.

Why should an essentially aristocratic place be so ill-kept, not to say dirty? The town is no centre of industry. Tall factory chimneys do not disfigure its silhouette or blacken its walls. Handsome equipages enliven the streets. But the municipality, like certain saints of old, seem to have taken vows of perpetual uncleanliness. Alike the scavenger's broom and the dust-cart appear to be unknown.

Whilst a riverside walk at Nevers presents nothing but cheerful bustle and an aspect of prosperity, here you approach the Allier through scenes of squalor and torpid neglect. The poorer inhabitants, too, are very un-French in appearance, wanting that personal tidiness characteristic of their country people in general. An aristocratic place, means an Ultramontane place, and every third man you meet in Moulins wears a soutane. What so many curés, Jesuits and Christian Brothers can find to do passes the ordinary comprehension.

However interesting twins may be in the human family, monumental duality is far from successful. Unfortunately for this delightfully picturesque old town, its graceful Cathedral has, in the grand new church of Sacre-Coeur, a double. But—

> *"As moonlight unto sunlight, and as water unto wine,"*

is the second self, the never to be obliterated shadow of the first and far more beautiful church.

Two towers of equal height, twice two spires like as cherries and in close juxtaposition rise above the town, an ensemble spoiling the symmetry of outline and general effect.

How much better off was Moulins when, instead of four spires, she gloried in two? Then, of a verity, the city would have presented as noble a view as those of La Charité and Nevers from the Loire.

The ancient château now used as a prison and the Jacquemart or clock tower are rare old bits of architecture, of themselves worth the journey to Moulins. Jacquemart, it may be here explained, is a corruption of Jacques Marques, the name of a famous Flemish clockmaker who lived in the fourteenth century. Amongst other achievements of this artist is the clock of Nôtre Dame, Dijon, as curious in its way as the still more celebrated cock-crowing time-piece of Strasburg, and declared by Froissart to be the wonder of Christendom. World-wide became the reputation of Jacques Marques, and thus it came about that clock towers generally were called after his masterpieces.

On my former hurried visit to Moulins, as was the case with my predecessor, Arthur Young over a hundred years before, "other occupations" had "driven even Maria and the poplar from my head, and left me no room for the Tombeau de Montmorenci." In other words, I had visited Rome without seeing the Pope.

On this second, and more leisurely visit, I had ample opportunity of making up for the omission. Truly, the tomb of the last Montmorency deserves a deliberate examination. It is one of the most sumptuous monuments in the world and as a testimony of wifely devotion worthy to be ranked with that of the Carian Queen to her lord, the Mausolus, whose name is perpetuated in the word mausoleum.

French history cannot be at everyone's fingers' ends, so a word here about the last of the Montmorencys, victim not so much of Richelieu's policy as of a kinsman's meanness.

When the dashing, devil-me-care, hitherto fortunate Henri de Montmorency, Marshal of France and Governor of Languedoc, plotted against Richelieu or rather against the Royal supremacy, it was mainly at the instigation of Gaston of Orleans. No more abject figure in French annals than this unworthy son of the great Gascon, Henri IV., thus portrayed by one whose tongue was as sharp as his sword: "Gaston of Orleans," wrote Richelieu, "engaged in every enterprise because he had not the will to resist persuasion, dishonourably drawing back from want of courage to support his associates."

In the conspiracy of Montmorency, Gaston had played the part of instigator, leaving the other to his fate as soon as the situation became perilous. Every effort was made to save the duke, but in vain, and at the age of thirty-seven he ended a brilliant, adventuresome life on the scaffold at Toulouse.

One thought was uppermost in my mind when, a few years ago, I visited that city, the only French city that welcomed the Inquisition. As I stood in the elegant Capitol, musing on Montmorency's story, it occurred to me how few of us realise what a respecter of persons was French law under the ancien régime. Hard as seems the fate of this dashing young duke, we must remember what would have been his punishment, but for his titles of nobility. Death swift and sudden, in other words, by decapitation, was the choicest prerogative of the nobility; tortures before and after condemnation, breaking on the wheel, burning alive, and other hideous ends, being the lot of the people.

This monument, so noteworthy alike from a historic and artistic point of view, was saved from destruction by ready wit. When, in the ferment of revolution, the iconoclastic spirit had got the upper hand, a citizen of Moulins met a mob, bent on destroying what they supposed to be the tomb of some hated grand seigneur, oppressor of the poor. Following the rabble to the convent, no sooner did he see the mallet and hammer raised than this worthy bourgeois, who himself deserves a monument, shouted, "Hands off, citizens! Yonder reposes no aristocrat, but as good a citizen as any man-jack of you, aye, who had the honour of losing his head for having conspired against a King."

The crowd melted away without a word, the monument remains intact, and generations have had bequeathed to them an example of what presence of mind may effect, not with nerve, sinew, or bodily prowess, but with the tongue. The Convent of the Visitation, to which Montmorency's widow retired, and in the chapel of which she raised this memorial, is now converted into a Lycée. It is a handsome building and was built by Madame de Chantal, foundress of the Order of Visitadines, or nuns whose office it was to visit the sick. This pious lady, the friend of St.

François de Sales, and herself canonised by Pope Benoît XIV., was the bosom friend of Felicia Orsini, Montmorency's wife, who succeeded her as Superior of the convent on her death.

But even an abbess, who had taken the veil, could not refuse visits, some of which must have been as a second entering of iron into this proud woman's soul. The coward Gaston, when passing through Moulins, sought an interview. Richelieu, also, whose emissary received the following message: "Tell your master, that my tears reply for me and that I am his humble servant." Years after, Louis XIV. visited the once beautiful and high-spirited Italian, now an aged abbess occupying a bare cell and from his lips, despot and voluptuary though he was, might always be expected the right word in the right place. "Madame," he said, on taking leave, "we may learn something here. I need not ask you to pray for the King."

{Illustration: TOMB OF MONTMORENCY, MOULINS.}

But interest in personalities is leading me from what I have set myself to describe, namely, portraiture in marble. For this magnificent work thus perpetuates the last of the Montmorencys and his wife as they were when separated for ever in their prime. Imposing although the monument is as a whole, these two figures in white marble, standing out against a dark background, engross attention. The entire work covers the wall behind the high altar, the sculptures being in pure white marble, the framework in black. Dismissing the niched Mars and Hercules on the one side, the allegorised Religion and Charity on the other, we study the central figures both offering interest of quite different kind.

Why a dashing soldier and courtier of the Renaissance should be represented in the guise of a Roman warrior, is an anomaly, irreconcilable as that of pagan gods and the personification of Christian attributes here placed vis-à-vis. Perhaps the grief-stricken wife, who was, as it appears, of a highly romantic and adventuresome turn, wished thus to commemorate the heroic qualities of her husband; she might also have wished to dissociate him altogether from his own time, a period of which, in her eyes, he would be the victim. Be this as it may, the Roman undress and accoutrements do not harmonise with a physiognomy essentially French and French of a given epoch. Whilst the interest aroused by the Duchess's effigy is purely artistic, that of her husband excites curiosity rather than admiration. The head is strangely poised, much as if the artist intended to suggest the fact of decapitation; obliquity of vision, a defect hereditary in the Montmorencys, is also indicated, adding singularity. The half-recumbent figure by the Duke's side, is of rare pathos and beauty. Almost angelic in its resignation and religious fervour is the upturned face. The drapery, too, shows classic grace and simplicity, as strongly contrasted with the martial travesty opposite as are the two countenances in expression.

Long will art-lovers linger before this monument raised by wifely devotion, a monument, with so many another, perpetuating rather the devotion of the survivor than claims on posterity of the dead. And let not hasty travellers follow Arthur Young's example, jotting down, after a visit to Moulins, "No room for the Tombeau de Montmorenci."

CHAPTER XII
SOUVIGNY AND SENS.

A quarter of an hour by rail, an hour and a quarter by road, from Moulins lies Souvigny, the cradle of the Bourbons, and as interesting and delightful a little excursion as travellers can desire. On a glowing September morning the scenery of the Allier looked its very best. Never as long as I live shall I forget the beauty of that drive. Lightest, loveliest cumuli floated athwart a pure, not too dazzlingly blue sky, before us stretched avenue after avenue of poplar or plane trees, veritable aisles of green letting in the azure, reminding me of the famous Hobbema in our National Gallery. At many points the landscape recalled our native land; but for the white oxen of the Morvan, we might have fancied ourselves in Sussex or the Midlands. And cloudage, to borrow an expression of Coleridge, suggested England, too. Clouds and skies of the Midlands, none more poetic or pictorial throughout England seemed here—those skies above the vast sweeps of undulating chalk having a peculiar depth and tenderness, the clouds a marvellous brilliance, transparence, and variety of form! So beautiful are those cloud-pictures that we hardly needed beauty below. Here on the road to Moulins we had both, the landscape, if not romantic or striking, being rich in pastoral charm. Arthur Young, who looked at every bit of country first and foremost from the farmer's point of view, was so much struck with the neighbourhood of Moulins that, but for the Revolution, he would very probably have become a French landowner. Just eight miles from the city he visited in August, 1789, an estate was offered for sale by its possessor, the Marquis de Goutte. "The finest climate in France, perhaps in Europe," he wrote, "a beautiful and healthy country, excellent roads, and navigation to Paris; wine, game, fish, and everything appears on the table except the produce of the tropics; a good house, a fine garden, with ready markets for every kind of produce; and, above all the rest, three thousand acres of enclosed land, capable in a very little time of being, without expense, quadrupled in its produce—altogether formed a picture sufficient to tempt a man who had been twenty-five years in the constant practice of husbandry adapted to the soil." The price of the whole was only thirteen thousand and odd pounds, and the seller took care to explain that "all seigneurial rights *haute justice*" (that is to say, the privilege of hanging poachers, and others, at the château gates), were included in the purchase money. But the country was already in a ferment, and had our countryman struck a bargain then and there, the last-named extras would have proved a dead letter. Seigneurial rights were being abolished, or rather surrendered, at the very time that this transaction was under consideration. As Arthur Young tells us, he might as well have asked for an elephant at Moulins as for a newspaper. No one knew, or apparently cared to know, what was taking place in Paris. On asking his landlady for a newspaper, she replied she had none, they were too dear. Whereupon the irate traveller wrote down in his diary: "it is a great pity that there is not a camp of *brigands* in your coffee room, Madame Bourgeau."

This part of France is not a region of prosperous peasant farmers, nor is it a chess-board of tiny crops, the four or five acre freeholds of small owners cut up into miniature fields. I had a long talk with a countryman, and he informed me that, as in Arthur Young's time, the land belongs to large owners, and is still, as in his time, cultivated by *métayers* on the half-profit system. At the present day, however, another class has sprung up, that of tenant farmers on a considerable scale; these, in their turn, sublet to peasants who give their labour and with whom they divide the profits. Now, the half-profit system does certainly answer elsewhere; in the Indre, for example, it has proved a stepping-stone to the position of small capitalist. Here I learned, with regret, that such is not the case. Land, even in the highly-favoured Allier, cannot afford a triple revenue. In the Indre, on the contrary, there is no intermediary between land-owners and *métayers*, the former even selling small holdings to their labourers as soon as they have saved a little capital.

"No; folks are not prosperous hereabouts," said my informant. "There are no manufacturers at Moulins to enrich the people, and, what with high rents and low prices, the half-profit system does not pay. If money is made, it is by the tenant-farmer, not by the *métayer*." Curious and instructive is the fact that the most Catholic and aristocratic centres in France should often be the poorest; Moulins and the Allier afford but one example out of many.

A beautiful drive of an hour and a quarter brought us within sight of Souvigny. Towering above the bright landscape rose the Abbey Church, its sober dun, red and brown hues, the quaint houses of similar colour huddled around it, contrasted with the dazzling brightness of sky and verdure.

Still more striking the contrast between the pile so majestic and surroundings so homely! Here, as at La Charité, nothing is in keeping with the mass of architecture, which, in its apogee, stood for the town itself, what of town, indeed, there was being the merest accessory, inevitable but unimposing entourage, growing up bit by bit. The present population of Souvigny is something over three thousand, doubtless, as in the case of La Charité, less than that of its former monastery and dependencies. As we wind upwards, thus flanking the town and abbey, we realise the superb position of this cradle and mausoleum of the Bourbons. For Souvigny was both. Two thousand and odd years ago, here, in the very heart of France, Adhémar, a brave soldier, nothing more, became the first "Sire de Bourbon," Charles le Simple having given him the fief of Bourbon as a reward for military services, its chief establishing himself at Souvigny, and of course founding a religious house. The Benedictine abbey, being enriched with the bones of two saints, former Abbots of Cluny, became a famous pilgrimage. Adhémar's successors transferred their seat of seigneurial government to Bourbon l'Archimbault, but for centuries here they found their last resting-place, and here they are commemorated in marble.

Indescribably picturesque is this whilom capital of the tiny feudal kingdom; topsy-turvy, higgledy-piggledy, coated of many colours are its zig-zag little streets, one house tumbling on the back of its neighbour, another having contrived to wedge itself between two of portlier bulk, a third coolly taking possession of some inviting frontage, shutting out its fellow's light, air, and sunshine; here, meeting the eye, breakneck alley, there aerial terrace, and on all sides architectural reminders of the Souvigny passed away, the Souvigny once so splendid and important, now reduced to nothingness, as is, politically speaking, the so-called House of France.

The Abbey Church, like that of La Charité, shows a mixture of many styles, the general effect being magnificent in the extreme. Throughout eastern France you find no more imposing façade.

But, as observes M. Emile Montégut, in the work before quoted, the church has been created as Nature creates a soil, each age contributing its layer; Byzantine, Roman, Gothic, each style is here seen, the latter in its purity.

Whilst the church itself stands taut and trim, a mass of sculptured masonry in rich browns and reds, the interior shows melancholy dilapidation. But, indeed, for the stern lessons of history, how sad were the spectacle of these mutilated effigies in marble, exquisite sculptures when fresh from the artist's hand, to-day torsos so hideously hacked and hewn as hardly to look human! We cannot, however, forget that the history of races, as of nations and individuals, is retributive. When the 'Roi-Soleil,' that incarnation of the Bourbon spirit, was so inflated with his own personality as to forbid the erection of any statue throughout France but his own, he paved the way for the revolutionary iconoclasts of a century later. It was simply a recurrence of the old fatality, the inevitable moral, since History began.

For here, defaced to such a point that sculptures they can be called no longer, are memorialised not only Louis XIV.'s ancestors, but his offspring, namely, Louise Marie, one of his seven children by Madame de Montespan, all, as we know, with those of Madame de la Vallière, legitimised, ennobled and enriched. Pierre de Beaujeu, husband of the great Anne of France, was also buried here. Anne it was who, on the death of Louis XI., governed France with all her father's astuteness, but without his cruelty, and pleasant and comforting it is to find that Duke Pierre, her husband, seconded her in every way, himself remaining in the background, acting to perfection the difficult rôle of Prince Consort. The sight of these once exquisite marbles may perhaps awaken in other minds the reflection that crossed my own. Heretical as I shall seem, I venture to express the opinion, that in such cases one of two courses are advisable, either the removal of the torsos, or restoration; why should not some genius be able in this field to do what Viollet le Duc has so successfully achieved in another? But for that great architect, the cathedral of Moulins—and how many other beautiful French churches?—would long ago have tumbled to pieces, been handed over as storage to corn merchants, or brewers! Is it so much more difficult to restore a marble effigy, whether of human being or animal, than a façade or an altar-piece? If impossible, then, I say, let broken marbles like those of Souvigny be hidden from view.

The agreeable town of Sens on the Yonne is here described for completeness' sake. Although not lying in the Bourbonnais, Sens formed the last stage of our little tour in this direction, a direct line of railway connecting the town with Moulins. What a change we found here! Instead of unswept, malodorous streets, and sordid riverside quarters, all was clean, trim, and cared for, one wholly uncommon feature lending especial charm.

For the tutelar goddess of Sens, benignant genius presiding over the city, is a stream, or rather parent of many streams, that water the streets of their own free will, supplying thirsty beasts with copious draughts in torrid weather, and keeping up a perpetual air of rusticity and coolness.

Wherever you go you are followed by the musical ripple of these runlets, purling brooks so crystalline that you are tempted to look for forget-me-nots.

The voluntariness of this street watering constitutes its witchery. Post haste flows each tiny course; not having a moment to spare seems every current. Need we wonder at the fabled Arethusas and Sabrinas of more youthful worlds?

Of itself Sens is very engaging. We can easily understand the fact of the late Mr. Hamerton having made his first French home here. In the memoir of her husband, affixed to his autobiography, Mrs. Hamerton gives us particulars, not only of individual, but of super-personal interest. I use the last expression because the idiosyncrasy described is common to most men and women of genius or exceptional talent. The charming essayist then, the art-critic, gifted with so much insight and feeling settled down at Sens we are told, for the purpose of painting 'commission pictures.' His career was to be decided by the brush and not by the pen. The author of "The Intellectual Life," with how many other works of distinction, had, at the outset, wholly mistaken his vocation. "The first thing considered by Gilbert when he settled at Sens," writes Mrs. Hamerton, "was the choice of subjects for his commission pictures, which he intended to paint directly from nature; and he soon selected panoramic views from the top of a vine-clad hill, called Saint Bon, which commands an extensive view of the river Yonne, and of the plains about it." Unfortunately, rather we should say fortunately, anyhow, for the reading world, the 'commission pictures' were declined. The disappointed artist, out of humour with Sens, made a series of journeys in search of an ideal home, the result being that most entertaining and successful book, "Round My House," and the final devotion of its author to letters.

Sens might well seem an ideal place of abode to many. Formed from the ancient Province of Burgundy, the Department of the Yonne has the charm of Burgundian scenery, with the addition of a wide, lovely river. All travellers on the Lyons-Marseilles Railway will recall the noble appearance of the town from the railway—the Cathedral, with its one lofty tower, rising above grey roofs, no factory chimneys marring the outline, and, between bright stretches of country, the Yonne, not least enchanting of French rivers, if not the most striking or romantic, perhaps the sweetest and most soothing in the world. The favourable impression of Sens gained by this fleeting view, is more than justified on nearer acquaintance. The Cathedral, externally less imposing than those of Bourges, Rheims, or even Rodez and Beauvais, is of a piece alike without and within, no tasteless excrescence disfiguring its outer walls, little or no modern tawdriness to be seen inside, an architectural gem of great purity. For the curious in such matters, the sacristy offers many wonders, among others a large fragment of the true cross, presented to Sens by Charlemagne. Less apocryphal are the vestments of our own Archbishop Thomas, alb, girdle, stole, and the rest, all most carefully preserved and exhibited in a glass case. It will be remembered that, when the turbulent Thomas of London, afterwards known as Becket, was condemned as a traitor, he fled to France. "This is a fearful day," said one of his attendants on hearing the sentence. "The Day of Judgment will be more fearful," replied Thomas. It was not at Sens, however, that the refugee took up his abode, but in the Abbey of St. Colombe, now in ruins hard by.

On the other side of the bridge, crowning an islet, stands one of those curious church*lets*, or chur*clings* I was about to say, that possess so powerful a fascination for the archaeological mind. Particularly striking was the little Romanesque interior in the September twilight, a picturesque group of Sisters of St. Vincent de Paul, rehearsing canticles with their pupils at one end, the subdued light just enabling us to realise the harmony of proportions. This little church of St. Maurice dating from the twelfth century, partly restored in the sixteenth, must not on any account be missed. Its pretty spire crowns the Isle d'Yonne, or island of the Yonne.

CHAPTER XIII
ARCIS-SUR-AUBE.

Late and tired, I arrived, one September evening, at Arcis-sur-Aube, birthplace and home of the great Danton.

I had brought with me letters of introduction to friends' friends, unaware that at such a moment the sign-manual of the President of the Republic himself would hardly have secured me a night's lodging. For at this especial moment the little town, from end to end, was in the possession of the military headquarters of that year's manoeuvres.

Every private dwelling showed a notice of the officers in command sheltered under its roof. Here and there, the presence of sentinels indicated the location of generals. The hotels were crowded from basement to attic, folks who let lodgings for hire had made bargains long before, whilst the very poorest made up beds, or turned out of their own, to accommodate the rank and file. At the extreme end of the town, close to the ancestral home of the Dantons, stands the straggling old-fashioned Hôtel de la Poste, a hostelry, I should suppose, not in the least changed since the days of the great conventionnel. All here was bustle and excitement. Mine host was spitting game in the kitchen, and could hardly find time to answer my application; soldiers and officers' servants, scullions and men of all-work, almost knocked each other down in the inn-yard, the landlady, generally so affable a personage in provincial France, gave me the cold shoulder. I turned out in the forlorn hope of finding a good Samaritan. Of course, to present a letter of introduction under such circumstances, was quite out of the question, my errand would have been the last hair to break the camel's back, final embarrassment of an already overdone hostess. But night was at hand; the last train to Troyes, the nearest town, had gone, no other would pass through Arcis-sur-Aube until the small hours of the morning. Unless I could procure a room, therefore, I should be in the position of a homeless vagrant. Well, not to be dismayed, I set out making inquiries right and left, to my astonishment being rebuffed rather surlily and with looks of suspicion. The fact is, during these manoeuvres, a lady arriving at head-quarters alone is apt to be looked upon with no favourable eye. Especially do people wonder what on earth can bring a foreigner to an out of the way country place at such a time—she must surely be a spy, pickpocket or something worse!

After having vainly made inquiries to no purpose along the principal street, I turned into a grocer's shop in a smaller thoroughfare; two young assistants were chatting without anything to do, and they looked so good-natured that I entered and begged them to help me.

Very likely an English hobbledehoy similarly appealed to would have blushed, giggled, and got rid of the stranger as quickly as possible; French youths of all ranks have rather more of the man of the world in them. The elder of the lads became at once interested in my case, and manifested a keen desire to be serviceable. Hailing a little girl from without, he bade her conduct me to a certain Mademoiselle D—— who let rooms and might have one vacant. The little maid, fetching a companion to accompany us—here also was a French trait; whatever is done, must be done sociably—took me to the address given; the demoiselle in question was, however, not at home, but the concierge said that, another demoiselle living near would probably be able to accommodate me, which she did. Before I proceed with my narrative, however, I must mention the ill fortune that befell my useful little cicerone.

On taking leave I had given her half a franc, a modest recompense enough as I thought. The following story would seem to show that the good people of Arcis have not yet become imbued with modern ideas about money, also that they have a high notion of the value of truth. To my dismay I learnt next morning that the poor little girl had been soundly slapped, her mother refusing to believe that she had come honestly by so much money; as my hostess observed, the good woman might at least have waited for corroboration of the child's statement. A box of chocolate, transmitted by a third hand, I have no doubt acted as a consolation.

Dear kind mademoiselle Jenny M—— How warmly she welcomed me to her homely hearth! My little purple rosette, insignia of an officer of Public Instruction of France, proved a bond of union. This excellent woman was the daughter of a schoolmaster who had himself worn the academic ribbon, a

French schoolmaster's crowning ambition. He had left his daughter, in comfortable circumstances, that is to say, she enjoyed an annuity of £40 a year, the possession of a large, roomy house, part of which she let, and half an acre of garden full as it could be of flowers, fruit and vegetables. We at once became excellent friends.

"Now," she said, "I am very sorry that my best bedroom is given up to soldiers, two poor young fellows I took in the other night out of compassion. You can, however, have the little back room looking on to the garden, it is rather in disorder, but you will find the bed comfortable. I cannot offer to do much for you in the way of waiting, having a lame foot, but a woman brings me milk early in the morning and she shall put a cupful outside your door; bread and butter you will find in the little kitchen next to your room."

I assured her that such an arrangement would suit me very well, as I had my own spirit lamp and could make tea for myself; then we went downstairs. The great difficulty that night was to get anything to eat. The soldiers had eaten every body out of house and home, she assured me there was not such a thing as a chop or an egg to be had in the town for love or money. Fortunately, I had the remains of a cold chicken in my lunch basket, and this did duty for supper, my hostess pressing upon me some excellent Bordeaux.

As we chatted, she mentioned the fact that two or three friends, much in the same situation as herself, occupied the little houses running alongside her garden.

"We are all old maids," she informed me.

"Old maids," quoth I, "how is that? I thought there were no single women out of convents in France."

"The thing," she said, "has come about in this way—we have all enough to live upon, and so many women worsen their condition by marriage, instead of bettering it, that we made up our minds to live comfortably on what we have got, and not trouble our heads about the men. We live very happily together, and are all socialists, radicals, *libres penseuses* and the rest. We read a great deal, and, as you will see to-morrow, my father left me a good library."

As we sat at table in the somewhat untidy kitchen, my fellow guests, the conscripts, came in, they were pleasant, civil young fellows belonging to different classes of life. One was a middle-class civilian from an industrial city of the north, the other a homely peasant, son of the soil.

These conscripts, however poorly fed in barracks, fare like aldermen during these manoeuvres, everybody giving them to eat and drink of their best. They had just dined plentifully, but for all that, managed to get down a bumper of wine immediately offered by Mademoiselle Jenny; a hunk of Dijon gingerbread they did evidently find some difficulty in getting through. We toasted each other in friendliest fashion, and the civilian, out of compliment to myself, drank to the health of the English army.

Next morning I fared no less sumptuously than a soldier during the manoeuvres. A savoury steam had announced game for our mid-day meal.

"Now," said my hostess, as she dished up and began to carve a fat partridge cooked to a turn—"this bird that came so àpropos, is a present from a great-nephew of Danton. He is the *juge de paix* here and a good neighbour of mine. We will pay him a visit this afternoon."

Of this gentleman, of Danton's home and family, I shall say something later on. We made a round of visits that day, but the *juge de paix*, who seemed to share the tastes of his great ancestor, was in the country in search of more partridges. Other friends and acquaintances we found at home; among these was a retired confectioner, who had once kept a shop in Regent Street, and had told Mademoiselle Jenny that she would be delighted to talk English with me.

Warmly welcomed I was by the portly, prosperous looking pastry-cook, who was reading a newspaper and smoking a cigarette in a well-furnished, comfortable parlour. But alas! thirty years had elapsed since his departure from England, and during the interval he had never once interchanged a word with any of my country-people. To his intense mortification, he had completely lost hold of the English tongue! Another acquaintance, an elderly woman, who seemed to be living on small independent means, had a curious house pet. This, once a pretty little frisking lamb, had now reached the proportions of a big fat sheep. So docile and affectionate, however, was the animal, and so attached had the good soul become to it, that a pet it seemed likely to remain to the end of its days; the creature followed its mistress about like a dog.

The little town of Arcis-sur-Aube, like many another, is now deserted by all who can get to livelier and more bustling centres. Tanneries, vest, stocking and glove weaving and stitching, are the only resources of the place.

During my stay, I made the acquaintance of a charming family engaged in the latter trade. Stopping one day in front of a weaver's open door to watch him at work, I was cordially invited to enter. The head of the house, one of those quiet, intelligent, dignified artisans so typical of his class in France, was weaving vest sleeves at a hand loom, just as I had seen, at St. Étienne, ribbon weavers pursuing their avocations at home. As we chatted about his handicraft and its modest emoluments, his little son came in from school, a bright lad who, to his father's delight, had lately gained prizes. It is curious that only one part of a vest, stocking or glove is done by a single hand; some goods I found came to this house to be finished and others were sent away to be made ready for sale elsewhere. By-and-by, a pretty, refined girl, the daughter of the house, came in and asked me if I would like to see what she was doing.

Forthwith she took me to a neat, cheerful little room upstairs overlooking a garden.

On a table by the open window was a hand-sewing machine, and her occupation was the ornamental stitching of silk and cotton gloves by machinery. The pay seemed excessively low I thought, I believe something like twopence per dozen pair, but the young machinist seemed perfectly contented and happy.

"It is pleasant," she said, "to be able to earn something at home and to live with papa and mamma and my little brother."

Before leaving, with the prettiest grace in the world, she begged my acceptance of a dainty pair of lavender silk gloves knitted by her own hands.

Some day I hope to revisit Arcis-sur-Aube, and meantime I hold occasional intercourse by post with my friends in Danton's town.

CHAPTER XIV
ARCIS-SUR-AUBE—(*continued*).

But by far the most interesting acquaintance at this most historic little town was the great-nephew of Danton. Middle-aged, unpretentious of aspect, yet with that unmistakable look partly of dignified self-possession, partly of authority, seldom absent from the French official, I looked in vain for any likeness to the portraits of his great kinsman. Yet perhaps in the stalwart figure, manly proportions and bronzed complexion, might be traced some suggestion of the athlete, the strong swimmer, the bold sportsman, whose mighty voice once made Europe tremble. The brother of this gentleman also lived at Arcis-sur-Aube, but was absent during my visit. The *juge de paix* and his family were on friendliest terms with my hostess, and he would often drop in for a chat.

From him and other residents I gathered some interesting particulars about the Danton family. The great tribune left two little sons, George and Antoine, who grew up and resided in their ancestral home, hiding themselves from the world. Their young step-mother it was whose memory, when on the way to the guillotine, evoked from Danton the only betrayal of personal emotion throughout his stormy career: "Must I leave thee for ever, my beloved," then, quickly recovering himself, cried "Danton, no weakness!"

Madame Danton married again and is lost sight of. One of Danton's sisters entered a convent, as it was supposed hoping to expiate by a life given up to prayer the crimes, as she deemed them, of her brother. Meantime, appalled by the shadow of their father's memory, George and Antoine decided to remain celibate, a pair marked out for solitude and obloquy.

"Let the name of Danton perish from the recollection of man," they said.

The elder, however, afterwards acknowledged and, I believe, legitimised a daughter according to the merciful French law. Mademoiselle Danton became Madame Menuel, and, strange as it may seem, at the time of my visit, this direct descendant of

Danton was still living. President Carnot had given her a small pension in the form of a *bureau de tabac* at Troyes, where she died in 1896, leaving a son, who some years ago was divorced from his wife, emigrated to Buenos Ayres, and has never been heard of since. It is supposed that he is dead. The two great-nephews have each a son and a daughter living.

The *juge de paix* and his brother are now among the most respected citizens of Arcis, and have lived to witness the rehabilitation of their great ancestor. Neither of the pair inhabit the house in which Danton was born, and to which he ever returned with joy and satisfaction.

A sight of Danton's house is sufficient to disprove the calumnies of that noble woman, but inveterate hater, Madame Roland.

From her memoirs we might gather that Danton was a poverty-stricken, pettifogging lawyer of the basest class. That Danton's family belong to the well-to-do upper middle ranks, we see from the object lesson before us. At the time of my visit, this large, roomy, well-built house, with coach-house, stables and half-a-dozen acres of garden, orchard and wood, was to let for 700 francs a year. But so low a rent now-a-days is no indication of its value a hundred years ago.

{Illustration: DANTON'S HOME AT ARCIS-SUR-AUBE.}

The owner of the house most kindly showed me over every part.

It is two-storeyed, plainly but solidly constructed, and evidently arranged, according to French fashion, for a combined tenancy. Two or three families could here well be accommodated under the same roof, each having separate establishments. I found myself in a covered carriageway, cool dark corridors leading to outhouses and stables, a wide staircase with handsome oak balustrade to upstair kitchen and bed-chambers, on either side of the ground floor were spacious salon and dining room, fronting town and river, water-mills and quays. In the vast kitchen was an enormous chopping block, suggestive of large family joints.

My kind cicerone allowed me to linger in Danton's bed-chamber. I now looked out from the window at which the fallen leader was often seen by his townsfolk during the last days of his stormy career. In his night-cap the colossal figure might be descried gazing out into the night, as if peering into futurity, trying to read the future. Did he perhaps from time to time waver in his decision to abide his doom? We know that again and again his friends urged him to seek safety in flight.

"Does a man carry his country on the sole of his shoe?" he retorted fiercely, but it may well be that he here envied weaker men. Danton's character was thoroughly French. His ambition was as he said to retire to Arcis-sur-Aube and there plant cabbages. A devoted son, husband and father, his affections were also centred upon others not of his blood and name. He tenderly loved his old nurse, and left her a small pension. Within the last thirty years, thanks to M. Aulard and his collaborators, the history of the Revolution has been written anew, or rather for the first time. The gigantic figure of Danton stands forth to-day in its true light, as the saviour of France from the fate of Poland, and as a founder of the democratic idea. He succumbed less because he was a rival of Robespierre than because he was a friend of humanity.

"I would rather be guillotined than guillotine," he repeated, and it was mainly his effort to stay the Terror that made him its victim.

The study adjoining contained that suggestive library of English, Spanish, Italian, and ancient classics of which his biographers have given us a catalogue, but which are now, alas! dispersed for ever.

The house stands conspicuous, rearing a proud front to the world, if world could be used appropriately of so quiet, humdrum a little place. A few hundred yards off we reach the Church, Hôtel de Ville and open square. In 1886, a monument to Danton was inaugurated here with much ceremony. A bronze statue represents the great tribune in the fiery attitude of an orator, pronouncing his immortal phrase:—

"De l'audace, encore de l'audace, toujours de l'audace!"

Arcis-sur-Aube is a little town of three thousand souls, within an hour's railway journey from Troyes. The river Aube (Alba), so called from its silveriness flows by Danton's house. In his time and up to the opening of the railways the place was a port of some importance. Boats and barges carried goods to Troyes, Bar-sur-Aube and other towns.

Of late years Arcis has been partially surrounded with pleasant shady walks greatly appreciated by the townsfolk. Regretfully I quitted my circle of acquaintances here, little dreaming under what interesting circumstances I should next meet Danton's great-nephew.

CHAPTER XV
RHEIMS.

The grandest of all the grand cathedrals in France has been so fully described elsewhere, that I will not attempt to do justice to the subject myself. During one of my numerous visits to Rheims, however, it was my good fortune to enjoy a very rare experience. On the occasion of President Faure's funeral, the great *bourdon* or bell, formerly only tolled for the death of monarchs, was now heard for the second time during the Third Republic. Standing under the shadow of that vast minster the sound seemed to come from east and west, from above and below, dwarfing the hum of the city to nothingness, as if echoing from the remotest corners of France. It was no heroic figure now knelled by the deepest-voiced bell in the country, but in the person of the Havre tanner raised to the dignity of a ruler, was embodied a magnificent idea, the sovereignty of the people and the overthrow of privilege. Never as long as I live shall I forget the boom of that great bell, and long the solemn sound lingered on my ears.

A few days later the interior of the vast Cathedral echoed with sound almost as overwhelming in its force and solemnity. A grand mass was given in honour of the dead President.

In front of the high altar stood a lofty catafalque, the rich purple drapery blazing with gold. The nave was filled with dazzling uniforms and embroidered vestments. In especially reserved seats sat the officers of the Legion of Honour, among these in civilian dress figuring the honoured citizen of Rheims who has ever retained English nationality, Mr. Jonathan Holden.

What with beating drums, clashing cymbals, blaring trumpets and pealing organ, the tremendous vault seemed hardly capacious enough for the deafening combination of sound. As a relief came the funeral march of Chopin, the more subdued strains seeming almost inaudible after the tumult of the moment before. Never surely had plebeian requiem so imperial!

The rich, artistic and archaeological treasures of Rheims are well known. I will now describe one or two sights which do not come in the way of the tourist.

One of these is the so-called "Maison de Retraite" or associated home for people of small means. The handsome building, with its large grounds, accommodating three hundred tenants, is neither a hotel nor a boarding establishment, least of all an almshouse.

Under municipal patronage and support the "Maison de Retraite" offers rooms, board, attendance, laundress and even a small plot of garden for the annual sum of £16 to £24 per inmate, the second sum procuring larger rooms and more liberal fare. Personal independence is absolutely unhampered except by the fact that the lodge gate is closed at 10 p.m. As most of the tenants of the home are elderly folks, such a rule is no hardship. One great advantage of the system is the protection thus afforded to single women and old people, and the immunity from household cares. Meals are taken in common, but otherwise intercourse is voluntary. The French temperament is so sociable, however, and chat is such a necessity of existence, that we saw many groups on garden benches, and also in the recreation and reading rooms. When the number of small *rentiers* is considered, i.e., men and women of the middle-class living upon a minimum income, we can understand the usefulness of this home. I learned that the establishment is self-supporting, the initiatory expense having been borne by the town and philanthropists.

We strolled about with one of the managing staff finding the inmates very sociable; one elderly gentleman invited us to sit down in his bit of garden, very proud, as he might well be, of all the flowers he had contrived to crowd into so small a space. We were also welcomed into some of the neat interiors, these varying in size according to the scale of payment. The class profiting by this associated home was evidently that of the small *bourgeoisie*.

Children there seemed to be none, one and all of the tenants being elderly widows, widowers, bachelors or spinsters. There were, however, a few married couples, who, if they preferred it, could cook their own meals at home. For single, middle-class women here was a refuge answering to the conventual boarding house of the upper classes.

Unmarried women in France are not nearly so numerous as in England, and I must say they may well envy their English and American sisters in spinsterhood. An unmarried French lady belonging to genteel society cannot cross the street unaccompanied till she has passed her fortieth year, nor till then may she open the pages of Victor Hugo or read a newspaper. Even in this "Maison de Retraite" special provision was made for the privacy of single ladies; whether they liked it or not they were expected to eat in a separate dining room, and meet for social purposes in a separate salon. As there is no limit to the emotional period and the age of sentiment, perhaps these safeguards of propriety are not wholly superfluous.

Of course the economy of such an arrangement is very great. Think of a respectable fairly-educated young woman getting what good old John Bunyan calls "harbour and good company," in other words, all the other necessaries of life, with society into the bargain, for £16 a year! The attendance is of course somewhat rough and ready. We saw a stalwart, rough-haired, rather masculine-looking female setting one of the dinner-tables with a clatter that would drive the fastidious to distraction. But the good soul had evidently her heart in her work, and I dare aver that single-handed she got through as much as three English housemaids with ourselves. Would such a scheme answer in England? I doubt it. The Anglo-Saxon character is the reverse of sociable, and class distinctions are so in-rooted in the English nature that it would be very difficult to get ten English women together who considered themselves belonging to precisely the same class.

Furthermore, are there with us many widows or spinsters of the same class enjoying even such small independent means as the sums above mentioned? In France, teachers, tradeswomen, female clerks and others, by dint of rigid economy, usually insure for themselves a small income before reaching old age. Fortunately habits of thrift are increasing in England, and our women workers have a larger field and earn higher wages. I had also the privilege of seeing the great wool-combing factory of our countryman Mr. Jonathan Holden, for upwards of forty years a citizen of Rheims. This town has been for centuries one of the foremost seats of industry in France. Mr. Holden's chimneys are kept going night and day, Sundays excepted, with alternating shifts of workmen. All the hands employed are of French nationality and—a fact speaking volumes—no strike has ever disturbed the amicable relations of English employer and French employed. The great drawback to an inspection of these workshops is the din of the machinery and the odour of the skins. But there is something that takes hold of the imagination in the perfection to which machinery has been carried. As we gaze upon these huge engines, only occasionally touched by a woman's hand, we are reminded of man, the pigmy guiding an elephant. We seem conscious, moreover, of what almost approaches human intelligence, so much of the work achieved appearing voluntary rather than automatic. The skins reach Rheims direct from Australia and are here dressed, cleaned and prepared for working up into cloth. If machinery is brought almost to the perfection of manual dexterousness, human beings attain the precision of machinery.

I saw a neatly dressed girl at work whose sole occupation it was to tie up the wool, now white as snow and soft as silk, into small parcels. The wool already weighed came down by a little trough, and as swiftly and methodically as wheels set in motion, the girl's fingers folded the paper and tied the string. I should not like to guess how many of these parcels she turned off in half a minute.

CHAPTER XVI
RHEIMS—(*continued*).

Rheims possesses a handsome theatre, the acquaintance of which I was enabled to make under exceptional circumstances. At the risk of appearing slightly egotistical, I will here describe an incident which has other than personal interest. My visit to Damon's country, the particulars of which were given in a former chapter, had an especial object, viz., the setting of a novel of my own having the great conventionnel for its hero. The story was dramatised by two French collaborators, one of whom was at that time stage manager of the Grand Theatre, Rheims. What, then, was my delight to see one morning placarded throughout the town the announcement of the Anglo-French play? A few days before the first representation I had witnessed a rehearsal, and as I was guided through the dusky labyrinths of the theatre I could realise the excessive, the appalling, combustibility of such buildings. It is difficult, moreover, for those who have never penetrated into such recesses—whose only acquaintance is with the representation on the stage—to imagine how gloomy and sepulchral "behind the scenes" may appear. However, by-and-by it was all cheerful enough, and the rehearsal, I must say, although of a tragedy, abounded in touches of humour. My friend and myself were accommodated with chairs just in front of the stage near the prompter, a very friendly personage, who was evidently interested in the fact of my presence. The actors and actresses dropped in one by one and we exchanged a cordial handshake. There was nothing theatrical about the dress or manners of these ladies, whose ages ranged from extreme youth to middle age. They all looked pleasant, lady-like, ordinary women, who might have quitted their housekeeping or any other occupation of a domestic nature. The men, too, impressed me agreeably as they greeted myself and their colleagues. Very amusing was the commencement of proceedings.

"Come, my children, put yourselves into position," said the stage manager, making corrections or suggestions as he went on; now somebody spoke too loud, and now somebody was too inarticulate, now an arm was held too forward, and now a leg dragged too much. Excessively diverting, also, the dummy show. In one scene of the play, a village schoolmaster is holding a class of little boys and girls. To-day, a row of chairs did duty for the scholars and were duly harangued, catechised, and even admonished with a cane. In another scene, a peasant woman appears with her donkey, to whom she confides a long tirade of troubles, the donkey for the moment being like the showman's hero in the famous story, "round the corner." A third and still more amusing piece of dumb show occurred later, when an ex-abbess acting as housekeeper to the village curé, let fall a basket of potatoes which were supposed to roll about the stage. All went well and the prompter, to whom I appealed for an opinion, assured me that I need be under no uneasiness, for the piece would go off like a house on fire.

In spite of that favourable prognostic an author's first night is always a nervous affair, especially when that author is a foreigner, and her piece a translation from the original.

However, everything went merry as a marriage bell, my kind friends filled several boxes, and perhaps one of the most interesting incidents of the evening was the fact that just underneath sat Danton's great-nephew with his clerk, who had come from Arcis-sur-Aube expressly for the occasion. Between the acts I went down and chatted with these two gentlemen, also with a French friend who had travelled from Dijon—a six hours' railway journey—in order to witness the piece. To the best of my knowledge now for the first time Danton figured on the French stage.

It must be confessed that the theatre on this especial night was not a crowded house. In the first place, three large soirées, which had been postponed on account of the President's funeral, coincided with the representation. In the second place, as a rule, the wealthier and more fashionable classes do not patronise provincial theatres, especially when residing within easy reach of Paris. However, the pit and gallery were packed, and loud was the applause with which the appearance of Danton in a blue tail coat, top boots and sash, and his vehement utterances were greeted.

It had never crossed my mind that under such circumstances an author would be called for; when, indeed, at the close of the piece, cries of "Auteur! auteur!" were heard throughout the theatre, my friends begged me to show myself. Which, proudly enough, I did, first saluting the sovereign people in the gallery, then bowing less beamingly to the scantier audience in the boxes, finally acknowledging the acclamations from the pit. If "Danton à Arcis" brought its author neither fame nor fortune, it certainly repaid her in another and most agreeable fashion. Two or three days later, a second representation of the piece at popular prices was given, and upon that occasion the house was full to overflowing.

The Grand Theatre, Rheims, is a very handsome building, and like most other provincial houses maintains a company of its own, although from time to time it is visited by the best Paris troupes.

Yet another uncommon recollection of Rheims must here be recorded. In September of last year, I witnessed such a spectacle as my military friends assured me had never before been afforded to the marvel-loving; in other words, the sight of a hundred and sixty thousand men—a host perhaps more numerous than any ever commanded by Napoleon—performing evolutions within range of vision.

By half-past five in the morning I was off from Paris with my host and hostess in their motor car for the Northern railway station. The day of the great review broke dull and grey, and deserted indeed looked the usually gay and lively Paris streets. We reached the station at five minutes to six, i.e., five minutes before the starting of our train, and at once realised the neatness with which the day's programme had been arranged, both by the railway companies and the Government. The tens of thousands of sightseers had been despatched to Rheims by relays of trains during the night, and the station was now kept clear for the numerous specials conveying members of the Senate, the Chamber, and the Press. Here, therefore, was no crowding whatever, only a quiet stream of deputies, wearing their tricolour badges accompanied by their ladies, each deputy having the privilege of taking two.

Precisely on the stroke of six, our long and well-filled train consisting of first-class carriages only steamed out of the station, taking the northern route and only making a short halt at Soissons. No sooner had we joined the Compiègne line than we realised the tremendous precautions necessary in the case of visitors so august; double rows of soldiers were placed at short intervals on either side of the railway and detachments of mounted troops stationed at a distance guarded the route. The arrangements for our own comfort were perfect. Our train set us down, not at Rheims, but at Béthény itself the scene of the review, a temporary station having been there erected. We were, therefore within a hundred yards or so of our tribune, or raised stage, and of the luncheon tents, roads having been laid down to each by the Génie or engineering body. Numbered indications conspicuously placed quite prevented any confusion whatever, and, indeed, it was literally impossible for anyone to miss his way. The only eventuality that could have spoiled everything, wet weather, fortunately held off until the show was over. The review itself was a magnificent spectacle, surely not without irony when we consider that this great military display, one of the greatest on record, was got up in honour of the first Sovereign in the world who had dared to propose a general disarmament! Another line of thought was awakened by the fact of our isolation. The specially invited guests of the French Government upon this occasion numbered three thousand persons, and it seemed that for the Czar, his train, and these, the great show was got up. The thousands of outsiders, sightseers, and excursionists, brought to Rheims by cheap trains from all parts of France, were nowhere; in other words, invisible.

Whether or no such spectators got anything like a view of the evolutions I do not know. I should be inclined to think that from the distance at which they were kept the moving masses were mere blurs and nothing more. From our own tribune, adjoining that of the Presidential party, we commanded a view of the entire forces covering the vast plain, surrounded by rising ground.

Amazing it was to see the dark immovable lines slowly break up, and as if set in motion by machinery, deploy according to orders. The vast plain before us was a veritable sea of men, an army, one would think, sufficient for the military needs of all Europe.

One striking feature of these superb regiments, cavalry as well as infantry, was the excellence of the bands. Never before had I realised the inspiriting thing that martial music might be. Another interesting point was that afforded by the cyclists, several regiments having these newly formed companies. Whenever a flag was borne past, whether by foot or mounted soldier, the cheering was tremendous, but it was reserved for a regiment of Lorrainers to receive a veritable ovation. Still so fondly yearns the heart of France after her lost and mutilated provinces! On the whole, and speaking as a naïve amateur, I should say that no country in the world could show a grander military spectacle. Enthusiasm reigned amongst all beholders, but there was no display of political bias or any discordant note. Cries of "Vive la France!" were as frequent as those of "Vive l'armée!"

Not a policeman was to be seen anywhere, the deputies keeping order for themselves. And not always without an effort! People would rise from their seats, even stand on benches, despite the thundered out "Remain seated!" on all sides. On the whole, and with this exception, nothing could surpass the general good humour. And when the splendid cortege filed by at the close, delight and satisfaction beamed on every face. M. Loubet was so dignified, folks said, Madame Loubet was so well dressed, the deportment of M. Waldeck Rousseau was perfect, M. Deschanel handsomer than ever, and so on, every member of the Czar's, or rather the President's, entourage winning approval. General André and M. Delcassé were very warmly received. The slim, pale, fastidious looking young man in flat, white cap, green tunic, and high boots, seated beside the portly, genial figure wearing the broad Presidential ribbon, set me thinking. How at the bottom of his heart does the Autocrat of All The Russias view these representatives of the great French Republic! How does he really feel towards France, the first nation of the western world to set the example of officially recognised self-government, the initiator of a system as opposed to Russian despotism as is white to black? Whatever may be the secret of this strange Franco-Russian alliance, it is apparently in the interest of peace, and, as such, should be warmly welcomed by all advocates of progress.

The luncheon was superabundant, consisting of wines, cold meat, and bread in plenty. The task of finding refreshment for three thousand people had been satisfactorily solved. The only thing wanting was water. It seems that upon such an occasion no one was expected to drink anything short of Bordeaux, Burgundy, or pale ale.

All the special trains were crowded for the return journey, made by way of Meaux, but everyone made way for everyone, and we reached Paris at eight o'clock, almost as fresh and quite as good-humoured as we had quitted it at dawn. If this great review was interesting from one point more than another, it was from the manner in which it displayed the wonderful organising faculty of the French mind. The most trifling details no more than the largest combinations can disconcert this pre-eminently national aptitude.

CHAPTER XVII
SOULAINES AND BAR-SUR-AUBE.

The first of these places mentioned is a Champenois village twelve miles from a railway station. From the windows of my friends' château I look upon a magnificent deer park, where during the oft-time torrid heat of summer delicious shade is to be found.

Far away vast forests bound the horizon, to the north a hot open road leading to Brienne-le-Château, where Napoleon studied as a military cadet; eastward, lies varied scenery between Soulaines and Bar-sur-Aube, there woodland ending and the vine country beginning.

On one especial visit during September, not even these acres of closely-serried forest could induce more than a suggestion of shadow and coolness. Although screened from view the sun was there. Throughout a vast region—half a province of woodland—folks breathed the hot air of the Soudan. The tropic temperature admitted of no exercise during the day, but after four o'clock tea we broke up into parties—drove, rode, strolled, called upon homelier neighbours, visited quaint old churches hidden in the trees or forest nooks, the solitude only broken by pattering of deer and rabbits, or nut-cracking squirrel aloft. Here and there we would come upon huts of charcoal-burner and wood-cutter, gamekeepers and foresters, too, had their scattered lodges; such signs of human habitation being few and far between.

We are here in the remnant of the great Celtic forest of Der. The straggling village of Soulaines is one long street, a little stream running behind the picturesque, timbered houses, many of these have outer wooden staircases leading to grange or storehouse. Church and presbytery, convent and Mairie were conspicuous.

In the opposite direction, another church rose above the horizon, the centre of what in France is called not a village but a hamlet. Bare as a barn seen from far and near showed this little church, and we often walked thither for the sake of its picturesque surroundings. The portal of the quaint old building is a mass of ancient sculpture, close round it being grouped a few mud-built, timbered, one-storeyed dwellings all of a pattern.

Even in France are to be found day labourers, only the very poorest, however, being without a cottage, plot of ground, a cow and of poultry their own. Many of their interiors are far neater and cleaner than those of the farm-houses, their occupants not being so tied to the soil from morning to night, not, in fact, incited to Herculean labours by the spur of larger possession. We visited one of the poorest villages hereabouts, of not quite a hundred souls, but of course, provided with church, school and Mairie. Many a group of potato diggers we saw in the exquisite twilight, suggestive of Millet, many a landscape recalling other masters. This handful of woodlanders—for the village is surrounded by forests—is perhaps as poor as any rural population to be found throughout France. Yet here surprises await us. Some of the better off hire a little land, keep cows, rear poultry, most likely in time to become owners of a plot. They are paid for harvest work in kind, several we talked to having earned enough corn for the winter's consumption—as they put it—our winter's bread. They are a fine, sunburnt, well-formed race and seem cheerful enough. In one of the poorest houses, a huge pipkin on the fire emitted savoury steam, and rows of small cheeses garnished the shelves. Good oak bedsteads, linen presses and old-fashioned clocks were general. Every mantel-piece had its framed photograph and ornamental crockery. New milk was always freely offered us.

Within the precincts of this hamlet we find ourselves in a bluish-green land of mingled wood and water; above the reedy marsh, haunt of wild fowl, willows grew thick; here and there the water flowed freely, its surface broken by the plash of carp and trout. At this season all hands hereabouts were busy with threshing out the newly garnered corn and getting in potatoes. The crops are very varied, wheat, barley, lucerne, beetroot, buckwheat, colza, potatoes; we see a little of everything. Artificial manures are not much used, nor agricultural machinery to a great extent, except by large farmers, but the land is clean and in a high state of cultivation. Peasant property is the rule; labouring for hire, the condition of non-possession, very rare. And whether the times are good or evil, land dirt cheap or dear, the year's savings go to the purchase of a field or two and, as a necessary consequence, to the consolidation of the Republic and the maintenance of Parliamentary institutions.

I will now say something of our neighbours. One of these was the parish priest, who had the care of between six and seven hundred souls. The fact may be new to some readers that a village curé, even in these days, receives on an average little more than Goldsmith's country parson, "counted rich on forty pounds a year." This curé's stipend, including perquisites amounted to just sixty pounds yearly, in addition to which he had a good house, large garden and paddock. But compare such a position with that of one of our own rectors and vicars!

The Protestant clergy in France are better paid than those belonging to the orthodox faith. Being heads of families, they are supposed, and justly, to need more. Let it not be imagined, however, that the priest receives less under the Republic than under the Empire. But the cost of living has increased.

Of course there are black sheep in the Romish fold as elsewhere; perhaps even the simplicity, learning and devotion to duty of the individual I here write of, are rare. Yet one cannot help feeling how much more money the Government would have at command with which to remunerate good workers in pacific fields if disarmament were practicable. This excellent priest, like other men of education and taste, would have relished a little travel as much as do our own vicars and curates their annual outing to Norway or Switzerland. What remains for recreation and charity after defraying household expenses and cost of a housekeeper out of sixty pounds a year?

Next, let me say a word about the *juge de paix* in France, as I presume most readers are aware, a modest functionary, yet better paid than that of a priest. The average stipend of a justice of the peace is about a hundred pounds a year, with lodging, but although his duties often take him far afield he is not provided with a vehicle, and must either cycle or defray the cost of carriage hire. I know many of these rural magistrates, and have ever found them men of education and intelligence. I, now, for the first time, found one well read in English literature, not only able to discuss Shakespeare and Walter Scott, but the latest English novel appearing in translation as a feuilleton. It is well that these small officials should have such resources. Tied down as they are to remote country spots, their existence is often monotonous enough, especially during the winter months.

It seems to be a canon of French faith that you cannot have too much of a good thing, anyhow in the matter of wedding festivities. Parisian society is beginning to adopt English saving of time and money, fashionable marriages there now being followed by a brief lunch and reception. Country-folks stick to tradition, preferring to make the most of an event which as a rule happens only once during a lifetime. Gratifying as was the experience to an English guest, especially that guest being a devoted admirer of France, I must honestly confess that my share in such a celebration constituted probably the hardest day's work I ever performed. Here I will explain that the bride's father was head forester of my host and hostess, the great folks of the place, and adored by their humbler neighbours. Château and cottage were thus closely, nay affectionately, interested in the important event I am about to describe, and this aspect of it is fully as noteworthy as the truly Gallic character of the long drawn out fête itself.

By nine a.m. horses and carriages of the château, adorned with wedding favours, were flying madly about in all directions conveying the wedding party to and from the Mairie for the civil ceremony. An hour later we were ourselves off to the village church, the house party including three English guests. The enormously long religious ceremony over, a procession was formed headed by musicians, bride and bridegroom leading the way, fifty and odd couples following and the round of the village was made. At the door of the festive house we formed a circle, the newly-wedded pair embracing everyone and receiving congratulations; this is a somewhat lachrymose ceremony. The marriage was in every way satisfactory, but the nice-looking young bride, a general favourite, was quitting for ever her childhood's home. After some little delay we all took our places in two banqueting rooms, the tables being arranged horse-shoe wise. Facing bride and bridegroom sat my host, the second room being presided over by the bride's father, of whom I shall have something to say later. Here I give the bill of fare, merely adding that the festive board was neatly, even elegantly, spread, and that every dish was excellent:—

Hors d'oeuvre   *Salade de saison*

Radis, beurre frais, Langue fumée   *Fruits*

Bouchées à la Reine	*Brioche. Nougat*
Daim, sauce chassuer	*Desserts varies*
Galantine truffée	*Vins*
Salmis de canards	*Pineau, Bordeaux, Champagne*
Choux-fleurs	*Café, Liqueurs.*
Dinde truffée.	

Looking down the lines of well-dressed people, all with the exception of ourselves belonging to the same rank as the bride, I could but be struck with the good looks, gentle bearing, and general appearance of everyone. As to the head forester, he was one of Nature's gentlemen, and might easily have passed for a general or senator. At the table sat several young girls of the village, each having a cavalier, all these dressed very neatly and comporting themselves like well-bred young ladies without presumption or awkwardness. During the inevitable pauses between dish and dish, one after another of these pretty girls stood up and gratified the company with a song, the performance costing perhaps an effort, but being got through simply and naturally. In the midst of the banquet, which lasted over three hours, two professionals came to sing and recite. From the breakfast table, after toasts,—the afternoon being now well advanced—we again formed a procession to the Mairie, in front of which *al fresco* dancing commenced. Add that this out-of-door ball lasted till a second dinner, the dinner being followed by a second ball lasting far into the small hours. Nor did the celebration end here. The following day was equally devoted to visits, feasts, toasts, and dancing. What a national heritage is this capacity for fellowship, gaiety, and harmless mirth!

Bar-sur-Aube lies twelve miles off and a beautiful drive it is thither from Soulaines. We gradually leave forest, pasture and arable land, finding ourselves amid vineyards. At the little village of Ville-sur-Terre, we one day halted at a farm-house for a chat, the housewife most kindly presenting me with two highly decorative plates.

As we approach Bar-sur-Aube we come upon a wide and beautiful prospect, wooded hills dominating the plain.

This little town is very prettily situated, and like every other in France possesses some old churches. Perhaps its most famous child is Bombonnel, the great panther-slayer, born close by, who died at Dijon and whose souvenirs bequeathed to me as a legacy I have given elsewhere. The son of a working glazier, he made a little fortune as hawker of stockings in the streets of New Orleans, returned to France, cleared the Algerian Tell of panthers, for a time enjoyed ease with dignity in Burgundy; on the outbreak of the Franco-German War in 1870, as leader of a thousand *francs-tireurs*, gave the Germans more trouble than any commander of an army corps, twice had a price of £1,000 set upon his head, was glorified by Victor Hugo, received the decoration of the Legion of Honour, and as a reward for his patriotic services several hundred acres of land in Algeria. A gigantic statue of Sant Hubert, the patron of hunters, now commemorates the great little man, for he was short of statue, in the cemetery of Dijon.

Bar-sur-Aube is connected with another notoriety, the infamous Madame de la Motte, the arch-adventuress, who, a descendant herself of Valois kings, proved the undoing of Marie Antoinette. As was truly said by a great contemporary:—"The affair of the Diamond Necklace," wrote Mirabeau, "has been the forerunner of the Revolution."

This Jeanne de Valois, rescued from the gutter by a benovolent lady of title and a charitable priest, presents a psychological study rare even in the annals of crime. Never, perhaps, were daring, unscrupulousness, and the faculty of combination linked with so complete a disregard to consequences. The moving spring of her actions, often so complicated and foolhardy, was love of money and display. It seemed as if in her person, was accumulated the lavishness of French Royal mistresses from Diane de Poitiers down to Madame Dubarry. There was a good deal of the Becky Sharp about her too, although there is nothing in her history to show that, like Thackeray's heroine, "she had no objection to pay people if she had the money." If, indeed, anything in the shape of ethics guided the most astoundingly ingenious swindler we know of, it was some such principle as this: she ought to have been at Versailles, there being received as a recognised Princess of the Royal House; since, through no fault whatever of her own, she was not, she had a perfect right to avenge herself upon royalty and society in general.

How she wormed herself into the confidence of the Cardinal de Rohan, a man of the world and of education, would seem wholly unaccountable but for one fact. The Prince Primate had faith in Cagliostro and his nostrums, and when an individual has recourse to astrologers and fortune-tellers, we are quite in a position to gauge his mental condition. Like Mdlle. Couesdon of contemporary fame, Cagliostro held intercourse with the angel Gabriel, but his occult powers and privileges far exceeded those of the Parisian lady-seer. He was actually in the habit of dining with Henri IV., and two days before the Cardinal's arrest made his client believe that he had just accepted such an invitation!

It had been Rohan's ambition to obtain the favour of the Queen and a foremost position at court, hence the readiness with which he fell into the trap. For "the Valois orphan," now Comtesse de la Motte, not only possessed great personal attractions, but an extraordinary gift of persuasiveness. Without much apparent trouble she made the Cardinal believe that she was in the Queen's favour, and indeed in her confidence. Having got so far the rest was easy.

How the acquisition of the already celebrated Diamond Necklace was first thought of, how, by the aid of willing tools, she matured and carried out her deep-laid and diabolical scheme, reads like an adventure from the "Arabian Nights." The personification of the Queen by a little dressmaker who happened to resemble her, the forgery of the Royal signature, the final attainment of the diamonds, all seemed so easy to this consummate trickster that it is small wonder she became intoxicated with success and blind to consequences. No sooner was the necklace in her possession than, of course, as fast as possible it was turned, not into money, but into money's worth. Houses and lands, equipages and furniture, costly apparel, and delicacies for the table were purchased, not with louis d'or, but with diamonds.

We read of her triumphant entry into the little town of Bar-sur-Aube, cradle of the Saint Rémy-Valois family, in a berline with white trappings and the Valois armorials, before and behind the carriage, which was drawn by "four English horses with short tails," rode lacqueys, whilst on the footboard ready to open the door stood a negro, "covered, from head to foot with silver." Still more dazzling was the dress of Madame la Comtesse, richest brocade trimmed with rubies and emeralds. As to the Count, not content with having rings on every finger he wore four gold watch chains! Besides holding open house when at home, the pair had a table always spread with dainties for those who chose to partake in their hosts' absence. Among the toys paid for in diamonds was an automatic bird that warbled and flapped its wings. This was intended for the amusement of visitors.

The carnival proved of short duration. It was on the 1st of February, 1783, that the diamond necklace was handed over to Madame de la Motte, Rohan receiving in return the forged signature of "Marie-Antoinette de France." On August of the same year, in the midst of a banquet given at Bar-sur-Aube, a visitor arrived with startling news. "The Prince Cardinal de Rohan, Grand Almoner of France, was on the Festival of Assumption, arrested in pontifical robes, charged with having purchased a diamond necklace in the name of the Queen."

The charm of these little French towns and rustic spots lies in their remoteness, the feeling they give us of being so entirely aloof from familiar surroundings. In many a small Breton or Norman town we hear little else but English speech, and in the one general shop of tiny villages see *The New York Herald* on sale. But from the time of leaving Nemours to that of reaching the farthest point mentioned in these sketches we encounter no English or American tourists. This essentially foreign atmosphere is not less agreeable than conducive to instruction. We are thus thrown into direct contact with the country people and are enabled to realise French modes of life and thought.

CHAPTER XVIII
ST. JEAN DE LOSNE.

Within the last twenty-five years so many new lines of railway have been opened in France that there is no longer any inducement—I am inclined to say excuse—for keeping to the main road. Yet, strangely enough, English tourists mostly ignore such opportunities. For one fellow-countryman we meet on the route described here, hundreds are encountered on the time-honoured roads running straight from Paris to Switzerland. Quit Dijon by any other way and the English-speaking world is lost sight of, perhaps more completely than anywhere else on the civilised globe. Again and again it has happened to myself to be regarded in rural France as a kind of curiosity, the first subject of Queen Victoria ever met with; again and again I have spent days, nay weeks, on French soil, the sole reminder of my native land being the daily paper posted in London. It is now many years since I first visited St. Jean de Losne, in company of a French acquaintance, a notary, both of us being bound to a country-house on the Saône. At that time the railway did not connect it with Dijon, and in brilliant September weather we jogged along by diligence, a pleasant five hours' journey enough. My companion, a native of the Côte d'Or, seemed to know everyone we passed on the way, whenever we stopped to change horses getting out for a gossip with this friend and that he had taken the precaution to provide himself with a huge loaf of bread, from which he hacked off morsels for us both from time to time. As we had started at seven o'clock in the morning, and got no déjeûner till past noon, the doles were acceptable. The fellow-traveller of that first journey—alas! With how many friends of the wine country!—has long since gone to his rest. The second time I set forth alone, taking my seat in the slow—the very slow—train running alongside the Canal de Bourgogne. On the central platforms of the Dijon railway station, crowds of English and American tourists were hurrying to their trains, bound respectively for Paris and Geneva. No sooner was I fairly off, my fellow travellers being two or three country-folks, than the conventionalities of travel had vanished. Surroundings as well as scenery became entirely French.

The Burgundian character is very affable, and although people may wonder what can be your errand in remote regions, they never show their curiosity after disagreeable fashion. They are delighted to discover that interest in France—artistic, economic, or industrial—has led you thither, and will afford any assistance or information in their power. They seem to regard the wayfaring Britisher as whimsical, that is all.

A train that crawls has this advantage, we can see everything by the way, villages, crops, and methods of cultivation. The landscape soon changes. The familiar characteristics of the wine country disappear. Instead of vine-clad hills, nurseries of young plants grafted on American stocks, and vineyard after vineyard in rich maturity, we now see hop gardens, colza fields, and wide pastures. Here and there we obtain a glimpse of some walled-in farmhouse, recalling the granges of our own Isle of Wight.

Alongside the railway runs the canal, that important waterway connecting the Seine with the Saône; but the Saône itself, Mr. Hamerton's favourite river, is not seen till we reach our destination.

The little town of St. Jean de Losne, although unknown to English readers, is one of the most historic of France. No other, indeed, boasts of more honourable renown. As Jeanne d'Arc had done just two centuries before, St. Jean de Losne saved the country in 1636. When the Imperial forces under Galas attempted the occupation of Burgundy, the dauntless townsfolk long held the enemy at bay and compelled final retreat. After generations profited by this heroism. Until the great year of 1789, the town, by royal edict, enjoyed complete immunity from taxation. On the outbreak of the Revolution, with true patriotic spirit, the citizens surrendered those privileges, of their own free will sharing the public burdens.

The first sight that meets the eye on entering St. Jean de Losne is the monument erected in commemoration of the siege. "Better late than never," is a proverb applicable to public as well as private affairs of conscience.

A little farther, and we reach the church of St. Jean. It contains a magnificent pulpit, carved from a single block of rich red marble, the niches ornamented with charming statuettes of the apostles. Close by is the Hôtel de Ville, in which are some interesting historic relics. As I passed through the courtyard, I saw an odd sight. One might have fancied that a second Imperial army threatened a siege, and that the townsfolk were laying in stores. The pavement was piled with bread and meat, whilst butchers and bakers were busily engaged in dividing these into portions, authorities, municipal, military and police, looking on.

I learned that these rations were for the regiments quartered in the town during the autumn manoeuvres. Every day such distributions take place; in country places the troops have recourse to the peasants, very often being treated as guests. A young friend, serving his three years, told me that nowhere had he found country folk more hospitable than in the Côte d'Or. No sooner did the soldiers make their appearance in a village, than forth came the inhabitants to welcome them, officers being carried off to châteaux, men by twos and threes to the home of curé or small owner. "Not a peasant," he said, "but would bring up a bottle of good wine from his cellar, and often after dinner we would get up a dance out of doors. On the saddle sometimes from two in the morning till twelve at noon, the kind reception and the jollity of the evening made up for the hardship and fatigue. We have just had several days of bad weather, and had to sleep on straw in barns and outhouses, wherever indeed shelter was to be had. Not one of us ever lost heart or temper; we remained gay as larks all the time."

An hour's railway journey from St. Jean de Losne takes the traveller to Lons-le-Saulnier, beautifully situated at the foot of the Jura range on the threshold of wild and romantic scenery.

A decade had not robbed this little town of its old-world look familiar to me, but meantime a new Lons-le-Saulnier had sprung up. Since my first visit a handsome bathing establishment has been built, with casino, concert-room, and all the other essentials of an inland watering-place. The waters are especially recommended for skin affections, gout, and rheumatism. Formerly the mineral springs of Lons, as the townsfolk lazily call the place, were chiefly frequented by residents and near neighbours. Improved accommodation, increased accessibility, cheapened travel and additional attractions, have changed matters. The season opening in May, and lasting till the end of October, is now patronised by hundreds of visitors from all parts of eastern France. These health resorts are much more sociable than our own. Folks drop alike social, political, and religious differences for the time being, and cultivate the art of being agreeable as only French people can. Excursions, picnics, and pleasure parties are arranged; in the evening the young folks dance whilst their elders play a rubber of whist, chat, look on, or make marriages. Many a wedding is arranged during the *Saison des Bains*, nor can such unions be called *mariages de convenance*, as in holiday-time intercourse is comparatively unrestricted. Grown-up or growing-up sons and daughters then meet as those on English or American soil.

Lons-le-Saulnier possesses little of interest except its Museum, rich in modern sculpture, and its quaint arcades, recalling the period of Spanish rule in Franche Comté. The excursions lying within easy reach are numerous and delightful. Foremost of these is a visit to the marvellous rock-shut valley of Baume-les-Messieurs, so called to distinguish it from Baume-les-Dames near Besançon. The descent is made on foot, and at first sight appears not only perilous but impracticable, the zigzag path being cut in almost perpendicular shelves of rock. This mountain staircase, or the "Échelle des Baumes," is not to be recommended to those afflicted with giddiness. Little sunshine reaches the heart of the gorge, yet below the turf is brilliant, a veritable islet of green threaded by a tiny river. The natural walls shutting us in have a majestic aspect, but playful and musical is the Seille as it ripples at our feet. Travellers of an adventuresome turn can explore the stalactite caverns and other marvels around; not the least of these is a tiny lake, the depth of which has never been sounded. For half-a-mile the valley winds towards the straggling village of Baume, and there the marvels abruptly end.

Nothing finer in the way of scenery is to be found throughout eastern France. In the ancient Abbey Church are two masterpieces, a retable in carved wood and a tomb ornamented with exquisite statuettes.

CHAPTER XIX
NANCY.

It is a pleasant six hours' journey from Dijon via Chalindrey to Nancy. We pass the little village of Gemeaux, in which amongst French friends I have spent so many happy days.

From the railway we catch sight of the monticule crowned by an obelisk; surmounting the vine-clad slopes, we also obtain a glimpse of its "Ormes de Sully," or group of magnificent elms, one of many in France supposed to have been planted by the great Sully. Since my first acquaintance with this neighbourhood, more than twenty years ago, the aspect of the country hereabouts has in no small degree changed. Hop gardens in many spots have replaced vineyards, owing to the devastation of the phylloxera. It was in the last years of the third Empire that the inhabitants of Roquemaure on the Rhône found their vines mysteriously withering.

A little later the left bank was attacked, and about the same time the famous brandy producing region of Cognac in the Charente showed similar symptoms. The cause of the mischief, the terrible Phylloxera devastatrix, was brought to light in 1868. This tiny insect is hardly visible to the naked eye, yet so formed by Nature as to be a wholesale engine of destruction, its phenomenal productiveness being no less fatal than its equally phenomenal powers of locomotion. One of these tiny parasites alone propagates at the rate of millions of eggs in a season, a thousand alone sufficing to destroy two acres and a half of vineyard. As formidable as this terrible fertility is the speed of the insect's wings or rather sails according extraordinary ease of movement. A gust of wind, a mere breath of air, and like a grain of dust or a tuft of thistledown, this germ of destruction is borne whither chance directs, to the certain ruin of any vineyard on which it lights. The havoc spread with terrible rapidity. From every vine-growing region of France arose cries of consternation. Within the space of a few years hundreds of thousands of acres were hopelessly blighted. In 1878 the invader was first noticed at Meursault in Burgundy; a few days later it appeared in the Botanical Gardens of Dijon. The cost of replanting vineyards with American stocks is so heavy, viz.: twenty pounds per hectare, that even many rich vintagers have preferred to cultivate other crops. Some owners have sold their lands outright.

On quitting Is-sur-Tille we enter the so-called Plat de Langres, or richly cultivated plains stretching between that town and Toul, in the Department of the Meurthe and Moselle.

With the almost sudden change of landscape—woods, winding rivers, and hayfields in which peasants are getting in their autumn crop, literally mauve-tinted from the profusion of autumn crocuses—we encounter sharp contrasts, the events of 1870-1 changing the French frontier, necessitating the transformation we now behold—once quiet, old-world towns now wearing the aspect of a vast camp, everywhere to be seen military defences on a wholly inconceivable scale. It is comforting to hear from the lips of those who should know, that at the present time war is impossible, the engines of warfare being so tremendous that the result of a conflict would be simply annihilation on both sides. After ten years' absence, and in spite of radical changes, the elegant, exquisitely kept town of Nancy appears little altered to me. The ancient capital of Lorraine is now one of the largest garrisons on the eastern frontier, but the military aspect is not too obtrusive. Except for the perpetual roll of the heavy artillery waggons and perpetual sight of the red pantalon, we are apt to forget the present position of Nancy from a strategic point of view.

Other changes are pleasanter to dwell on. The Facultés, or schools of medicine, science, and law, removed hither from Strasburg after the annexation, have immensely increased the intellectual status of Nancy, whilst from the commercial and industrial side the advance has been no less. Its population has doubled since the events of 1870-1, and is constantly increasing. Why so few English travellers visit this dainty and attractive little capital is not easy to explain. More interesting even than the artistic and historic collections of Nancy is the celebrated School of Forestry. Formerly a few young Englishmen were out-students of this school, but since the study had been made accessible at home the foreign element at the time of my visit, consisted of a few Roumanians, sent by their Government. The École Forestière, courteously shown to visitors, was founded sixty years ago and is conducted on almost a military system. Only twenty-four students are received annually, and these must have passed severe examinations either at the École Agronomique of Paris, or at the École Polytechnique. The staff consists of a director and six professors, all paid by the State. Two or three years form the curriculum and successful students are sure of obtaining good Government appointments. Forestry being a most important service, every branch of natural science connected with the preservation of forests, and afforesting is taught, the school collections forming a most interesting and wholly unique museum. Here we see, exquisitely arranged as books on library shelves, specimens of wood of all countries, whilst elsewhere sections from the tiniest to the gigantic stems of America. Very instructive, too, are the models of those regions in France already afforested, and of those undergoing the process; we also see the system by means of which the soil is so consolidated as to render plantation possible, namely, the arresting of mountain torrents by dams and barrages. In the Dauphiné, and French Alps generally, many denuded tracks are in course of transformation, the expense being partly borne by the State and partly by the communes. It is impossible to over-estimate the importance of such works, alike from a climatic, economic, and hygienic point of view. The extensive eucalyptus plantations in Algeria, teach us the value of afforesting, vast tracks having been thereby rendered healthful and cultivable.

A strikingly beautiful city, sad of aspect withal, is this ancient capital of Lorraine, ever wearing half mourning, as it seems, for the loss of its sister Alsace.

Unforgettable is the glimpse of the Place Stanislas, with its bronze gates, fountains, and statue, worthy of a great capital; of the beautiful figure of Duke Antonio of Lorraine on horseback, under an archway of flamboyant Gothic; of the Ducal Palace and its airy colonnade; lastly, of the picturesque old city gate, the Porte de la Crafie, one of the most striking monuments of the kind in France.

All these things may be glanced at in an hour, but in order to enjoy Nancy thoroughly, a day or two should be devoted to it, and creature comforts are to be had in the hotels.

In the Ducal Palace are shown the rich tapestries found in the tent of Charles le Téméraire after his defeat before Nancy, and other relics of that Haroun-al-Raschid of his epoch, who bivouacked off gold and silver plate, and wore on the battle-field diamonds worth half a million. The cenotaphs of the Dukes of Lorraine are in a little church outside the town—the *chapelle ronde*, as the splendid little mausoleum is designated, its imposing monuments of black marble and richly-decorated octagonal dome, making up a solemn and beautiful whole. Graceful and beautiful also are the monuments in the church itself, and those of another church, des Cordeliers, close to the Ducal Palace.

Nancy is especially rich in monumental sculpture, but it is in the cathedral that we are enchanted by the marble statues of the four doctors of the church—St. Augustine, St. Grégoire, St. Léon, and St. Jerome. These are the work of Nicholas Drouin, a native of the town, and formerly ornamented a tomb in the church of the Cordeliers just mentioned. The physiognomy, expression, and pose of St. Augustine are well worthy of a sculptor's closest study, but it is rather as a whole than in detail that this exquisite statue delights the ordinary observer.

All four sculptures are noble works of art; the beautiful, dignified figure of St. Augustine somehow takes strongest hold of the imagination. We would fain return to it again and again, as indeed we would fain return to all else we have seen in the fascinating city of Nancy.

From Nancy, by way of Epinal, we may easily reach the heart of the Vosges.

CHAPTER XX
IN GERMANISED LORRAINE.

At the railway station of Nancy, I was met by a French family party, my hosts to be in a château on the other side of the French frontier.

We had jogged on pleasantly enough for about half an hour, when the gentlemen of the party, with (to me) perplexing smiles, briskly folded their newspapers and consigned them, not to their pockets or rugs, but to their ladies, by whom the journals were secreted in underskirts.

"We are approaching the frontier," said Madame to me.

I afterwards learned that only one or two French newspapers are allowed to circulate in the annexed provinces, the *Temps* and others, the names of which I forget; for the first and second offence of smuggling prohibited newspapers, the offender is subjected to a reprimand, the third offence is punished by a fine, the fourth involves imprisonment. Now, as all of us know who have lived in France, the *Figaro* is a veritable necessity to the better-off classes in France, the *Times* to John Bull not more so. Similarly, to the peasant and the artisan, the *Petit Journal* takes the place of the half-penny newspaper in England. This deprivation is cruelly felt, and is part of the system introduced by William II.

Custom-house dues are at all times vexatious, but on the French-Prussian frontier they are so arranged as to provoke patriotic feeling. It may seem a foolish fancy for French folks, German subjects of the Kaiser, to prefer French soap and stationery, yet what more natural than the purchase of such things when within easy reach? Thus, on alighting at the frontier, not only were trunks and baskets turned out, we were all eyed from head to foot suspiciously. My hosts' newspapers were not unearthed, certainly; perhaps their rank and position counted for something. But one country girl had to pay duty on a shilling box of writing paper, another was mulcted to half the value of a bottle of scent, and so on. There was something really pathetic in the forced display of these trifles, the purchasers being working people and peasants. All French goods and productions are exorbitantly taxed. Thus a lady must pay three or four shillings duty on a bonnet perhaps costing twenty in France. On a cask of wine, the duty often exceeds the price of its contents, and, according to an inexorable law of human nature, the more inaccessible are these patriotic luxuries, so the more persistently will they be coveted and indulged in.

Custom House officials on the Prussian side have no easy time of it, ladies especially giving them no little trouble. The duty on a new dress sent or brought from France across the frontier is ten francs; and we were told an amusing story of a French lady, who thought to neatly circumvent the douane. She was going from Nancy to Strasburg to a wedding, and in the ladies' waiting-room on the French side changed her dress, putting on the new, a rich costume bought for the ceremony. The officials got wind of the matter. The dress was seized and finally redeemed after damages of a thousand francs!

Persons in indifferent circumstances, however patriotic they may be, can subsist upon German beer, soap, and writing paper. The blood tax, upon which I shall say something further on, is a wholly different matter.

A short drive brought us to a noble château, inside a beautifully wooded park, the iron gateway showing armorial bearings. Indoors there was nothing to remind me that I had exchanged Republican France for autocratic Prussia. Guests, servants, speech, usages, books, were French, or, in the case of the three latter, English. Every member of the family spoke English, afternoon tea was served as at home, and the latest Tauchnitz volumes lay on the table.

Difficult indeed it seemed to realise that I had crossed the frontier, that though within easy reach, almost in sight of it, the miss, alas! Was as good as a mile.

Alsace-Lorraine, I may here mention, is a verbal annexation dating from 1871. Whilst Alsace was German until its conquest by Louis XIV., Lorraine, the country of Jeanne d'Arc, had been in part French and French-speaking for centuries. Alsace under French *régime* retained alike Protestantism and Teutonic speech. We can easily understand that the changes of 1871 should come much harder to the Catholic Lorrainers than to their Protestant Alsatian neighbours.

Bitterness of feeling does not seem to me to diminish with time. On the occasion of my third visit to Germanised France, I found things much the same, the clinging to France ineradicable as ever, nothing like the faintest sign of reconciliation with Imperial rule.

One might suppose that, after a generation, some slight approach to intercourse would exist among the French and Prussian populations. By the upper classes the Germans, no matter what their rank or position, remain tabooed as were Jews in the Ghetto of former days.

At luncheon next day, my host smilingly informed me that he had filled up the paper left by the commissary of police, concerning their newly arrived English visitor. We are here, it must be remembered, in a perpetual state of siege.

"I put down Canterbury as your birthplace—" he began.

"Good Heavens!" exclaimed I, "I was born near Ipswich."

"Oh!" he said, smiling, "I just put down the first name that occurred to me, and filled in particulars as to age, etc.," here he bowed, "after a fashion which I felt would be satisfactory to yourself."

This kind of domiciliary visit may appear a joking matter, but to live under a state of siege is no subject for pleasantry, as I shall show further on. Here is another instance of the comic side of annexation, if the adjective could be applied to such a subject. In the salon I noticed a sofa cushion, covered, as I thought to my astonishment, with the Prussian flag. But my hostess smilingly informed me that, as the Tricolour was forbidden in Germanised Lorraine, by way of having the next best thing to it, she had used the Russian colours, symbol of the new ally of France.

Another vexation of unfortunate *annexés* is in the matter of bookbinding. French people naturally like to have their books bound in French style, but it is next to impossible to get this done in Alsace. If the books are bound in France, there is the extra cost of carriage and duty.

A very pleasant time I had under this French roof on German soil. Our days were spent in walks and drives, our evenings entertained with music and declamation. Now we had the Kreutzer Sonata exquisitely performed by amateur musicians, now we listened to selections from Lamartine, Nadaud, Victor Hugo and others, as admirably rendered by a member of this accomplished family, all the members of which were now gathered together. I saw something alike of their poorer and richer neighbours, all of course being their country-people. This social circle, including the household staff, was rigorously French.

Let me now describe a Lorraine lunch, as the French *goûter* or afternoon collation is universally called, our hosts being a family of peasant farmers, their guests the house party from the château. We had only to drive a mile or two before quitting annexed France for France proper, the respective frontiers indicated by tall posts bearing the name and eagle of the German Empire and the R.F. of France.

"You are now on French soil," said my host to me with a smile of satisfaction, and the very horses seemed to realise the welcome fact. Right merrily they trotted along, joyfully sniffing the air of home.

The Lorraine villages are very unlike their spick and span neighbours of Alsace, visited by me two years before. Why Catholic villages should be dirty and Protestant ones clean, I will not attempt to explain. Such, however, is the case. As we drove through the line of dung-heaps and liquid manure rising above what looked like barns, I was ill-prepared for the comfort and tidiness prevailing within. What a change when the door opened, and our neatly dressed entertainers ushered us into their dining-room! Here, looking on to a well-kept garden was a table spread with spotless linen, covers being laid as in a middle-class house. An armchair, invariable token of respect, was placed for the English visitor; then we sat down to table, two blue-bloused men, uncle and nephew, and three elderly women in mob caps and grey print gowns, dispensing hospitality to their guests, belonging to the *noblesse* of Lorraine. There was no show of subservience on the one part, or of condescension on the other. Conversation flowed easily and gaily as at the château itself.

I here add that whilst the French *noblesse* and *bourgeoisie* remain apart as before the Revolution, with the peasant folk it is not so. These good people were not tenants or in any way dependents on my hosts. They were simply humble friends, the great tie being that of nationality. The order of the feast was peculiar. Being Friday no delicacy in the shape of a raised game pie could be offered; we were, therefore, first of all served with bread and butter and *vin ordinaire*. Then a dish of fresh honey in the comb was brought out; next, a huge open plum tart. When the tart had disappeared, cakes of various kinds and a bottle of good Bordeaux were served; finally, grapes, peaches, and pears with choice liqueurs. Healths were drunk, glasses chinked, and when at last the long lunch came to an end, we visited dairy, bedrooms, and garden, all patterns of neatness. This family of small peasant owners is typical of the very best rural population in France. The united capital of the group—uncle, aunts and nephew—would not perhaps exceed a few thousand pounds, but the land descending from generation to generation had increased in value owing to improved cultivation. Hops form the most important crop hereabouts. This village of French Lorraine testified to the educational liberality of the Republic. For the three hundred and odd souls the Government here provides schoolmaster, schoolmistress, and a second female teacher for the infant school, their salaries being double those paid under the Empire.

Now a word concerning the blood-tax. Rich and well-to-do French residents in the annexed provinces can afford to send their sons across the frontier and pay the heavy fines imposed for default. With the artisan and peasant the case is otherwise. Here defection from military service means not only lifelong separation but worldly ruin. To the wealthy an occasional sight of their young soldiers in France is an easy matter. A poor man must stay at home. If his sons quit Alsace-Lorraine in order to go through their military service on French soil, they cannot return until they have attained their forty-fifth year, and the penalty of default is so high that it means, and is intended to mean, ruin. There is also another crying evil of the system. French conscripts forced into the German Army are always sent as far as possible from home. If they fall ill and die, kith or kin can seldom reach them. Again, as French is persistently spoken in the home, and German only learnt under protest at the primary school, the young *annexé* enters upon his enforced military service with an imperfect knowledge of the latter language, the hardships of his position being thereby immensely enhanced. No one here hinted to me of any especial severity being shown to French conscripts on this account, but we can easily understand the disadvantage under which they labour. I visited a tenant farmer on the other side of the frontier, whose only son had lately died in hospital at Berlin. The poor father was telegraphed for but arrived too late, the blow saddening for ever an honest and laborious life. This farmer was well-to-do, but had other children. How then could he pay the fine imposed upon the defaulter? And, of course, French service involved lifelong separation. Cruel, indeed, is the dilemma of the unfortunate *annexé*. But the blood-tax is felt in other ways. During my third stay in Germanised Lorraine the autumn manoeuvres were taking place. This means that alike rich and poor are compelled to lodge and cook for as many soldiers as the authorities choose to impose upon them. I was assured by a resident that poor people often bid the worn-out men to their humble board, the conscripts' fare being regulated according to the strictest economy. In rich houses, German officers receive similar hospitality, but we can easily understand under what conditions.

The annexed provinces are of course being Germanised by force. Immigration continues at a heavy cost. Here is an instance in point.

When Alsace was handed over to the German Government it boasted of absolute solvency. It is now burdened with debt, owing, among many other reasons, to the high salaries received by the more important German officials; the explanation of this being that the position of these functionaries is so unpleasant they have to be bribed into such expatriation. Thus their salaries are double what they were under French rule. Not that friction often occurs between the German civil authorities and French subjects; everyone bears witness to the politeness of the former, but it is impossible for them not to feel the distastefulness of their own presence. On the other hand, the perpetual state of siege is a grievance daily felt. Free speech, liberty of the press, rights of public meeting, are unknown. Not long since, a peasant just crossed the frontier, and as he touched French soil, shouted "Vive la France!" On his return he was convicted of *lèse majesté* and sent to prison. Another story points to the same moral. At a meeting of a village council an aged peasant farmer, who cried "We are not subjects but servants of William II." Was imprisoned for six weeks. The occasion that called forth the protest was an enforced levy for some public works of no advantage whatever to the inhabitants. Sad indeed is the retrospect, sadder still the looking forward, with which we quit French friends in the portions of territory now known as Alsace-Lorraine. And when we say "Adieu" the word has additional meaning. Epistolary intercourse, no more than table-talk, is sacred.

CHAPTER XXI
IN GERMANISED ALSACE.

Who would quit Alsace without a pilgrimage to Saverne and the country home in which Edmond About wrote his most delightful pages and in which he dispensed such princely hospitality? The author of "Le Fellah " was forced to forsake his beloved retreat after the events of 1870-1; the experiences of this awful time are given in his volume "Alsace," and dedicated to his son—*pour qu'il se souvienne*—in order that he might remember. Here also as under that Lorraine roof I felt myself in France. At the time of my visit the property was for sale. French people, however, are loth to purchase estates in the country they may be said to inhabit on sufferance, while rich Germans prefer to build palatial villas within the triple fortifications and thirteen newly constructed forts which are supposed to render Strasburg impregnable.

The railway takes us from Strasburg in an hour to the picturesque old town of Saverne, beautifully placed above the Zorn. Turning our backs upon the one long street winding upwards to the château, we follow a road leading into the farthermost recesses of the valley, from which rise on either side the wooded spurs of the lower Vosges. Here in a natural *cul-de-sac*, wedged in between pine-clad slopes, is as delightful a retreat as genius or a literary worker could desire. On the superb September day of my visit the place looked its best, and warm was the welcome we received from the occupiers, a cultivated and distinguished French Protestant family, formerly living at Srasburg, but since the events of 1870-1 removed to Nancy. They hired this beautiful place from year to year, merely spending a few weeks here during the Long Vacation. The intellectual atmosphere still recalled bygone days, when Edmond About used to gather round him literary brethren, alike French and foreign. Pleasant it was to find here English-speaking, England-loving, French people. Nothing can be simpler than the house itself, in spite of its somewhat pretentious tower of which About wrote so fondly. His study is a small, low-pitched room, not too well lighted, but having a lovely outlook; beyond, the long, narrow gardens, fruit, flower and vegetable, one leading out of another, rising pine woods and the lofty peaks of the Vosges. So remote is this spot that wild deer venture into the gardens, whilst squirrels make themselves at home close to the house doors. Our host gave me much information about the peasants. Although not nearly so prosperous as before the annexation, they are doing fairly well. Some, indeed, are well off, possessing capital to the amount of several thousand pounds, whilst a millionaire, that is, the possessor of a million francs or forty thousand pounds, is found here and there. The severance from France entailed, however, one enormous loss on the farmer. This was the withdrawal of tobacco culture, a monopoly of the French State which afforded maximum profits to the cultivator. With regard to the indebtedness of the peasant-owner, my informant said that it certainly existed, but not to any great extent, usury having been prohibited by the local Reichstag a few years before. Again I found myself among French surroundings, French traditions, French speech. Let me add, however, that I heard none of the passionate regrets, recriminations, and wishes that had constantly fallen on my ears ten years before. One prayer, and one only, seems in every heart, on every lip, "Peace, peace—only let us have peace!" It must be borne in mind that 20,000 French Alsatians quitted Strasburg alone, and that those of the better classes who were unable to emigrate sent their young sons across the frontier before the age of seventeen. Thus, by a gradual process, the French element is being eliminated from the towns, whilst in the country annexation came in a very different guise.

This will be seen from the account of another excursion made with French friends living in Strasburg.

It is a beautiful drive to Blaesheim, southwest of the city, in a direct line with the Vosges and Oberlin's country. We pass the enormous public slaughterhouses and interminable lines of brand-new barracks, then under one of the twelve stone gates with double portals that now protect the city, leaving behind us the tremendous earthworks and powder magazines, and are soon in the open plain. This vast plain is fertile and well cultivated. On either side we see narrow, ribbon-like strips of maize, potatoes, clover, hops, beetroot, and hemp. There are no apparent boundaries of the various properties and no trees or houses to break the uniformity. The farm-houses and premises, as in the Pyrenees, are grouped together, forming the prettiest, neatest villages imaginable. Entzheim is one of these. The broad, clean street, the large white-washed timber houses, with projecting porches and roofs, may stand for a type of the Alsatian "Dorf." The houses are white-washed outside once a year, the mahogany-coloured rafters, placed crosswise, forming effective ornamentation. No manure heaps before the door are seen here, as in Brittany, all is clean and sightly. We meet numbers of pedestrians, the women mostly wearing the Alsatian head-dress, an enormous bow of broad black ribbon with long ends, worn fan-like on the head, and lending an air of great severity. The remainder of the costume—short blue or red skirt (the colours distinguishing Protestant and Catholic), gay kerchief, and apron—have all but vanished. As we approach our destination the outlines of the Vosges become more distinct, and the plain is broken by sloping vineyards and fir woods. We see no labourers afield, and, with one exception, no cattle. It is strange how often cattle are cooped up in pastoral regions. The farming here is on the old plan, and milch cows are stabled from January to December, only being taken out to water. Agricultural machinery and new methods are penetrating these villages at a snail's pace. The division of property is excessive. There are no lease-holds, and every farmer, alike on a small or large scale, is an owner.

Two classes in Alsace have been partly won over to the German rule; one is that of the Protestant clergy, the other that of the peasants.

The Third Empire persistently snubbed its Protestant subjects, then, as at the time of the Revocation, numbering many most distinguished citizens. No attempts, moreover, were made to Gallicise the German-speaking population of the Rhine provinces. Thus the wrench was much less felt here than in Catholic, French-speaking Lorraine. Higher stipends, good dwelling-houses and schools, have done much to soften annexation to the clergy. An afternoon "at home" in a country parsonage a few miles from Strasburg, reminded me of similar functions in an English rectory.

At the parsonage of Blaesheim we were warmly welcomed by friends, and in their pretty garden found a group of ladies and gentlemen playing at croquet, among them two nice-looking girls wearing the Alsatian *coiffe* that enormous construction of black ribbon just mentioned. These young ladies were daughters of the village mayor, a rich peasant, and had been educated in Switzerland, speaking French correctly and fluently. Many daughters of wealthy peasants marry civilians at Strasburg, when they for once and for all cast off the last feature of traditional costume. After a little chat, and being bidden to return to tea in half an hour, we visited some other old acquaintances of my friends, a worthy peasant family residing close by. Here also a surprise was in store for me. The head of the house and his wife—both far advanced in the sixties and who might have walked out of one of Erckman-Chatrian's novels—could not speak a word of French, although throughout the best part of their lives they had been French subjects!

Admirable types they were, but by no means given to sentiment or romance. The good man assured me in his quaint patois that he did not mind whether he was French, German, or, for the matter of that, English, so long as he could get along comfortably and peacefully! He added, however, that under the former *régime* taxes had been much lower and farming much more profitable. The good folk brought out bread and wine, and we toasted each other in right hearty fashion. Over the sideboard of their clean, well-furnished sitting room hung a small photograph of William II. On our return to our first host we found a sumptuous five o'clock tea prepared for the ladies, whilst more solid refreshments awaited the gentlemen in the garden.

Even in a remote corner of Alsace, memorialized by Germany's greatest poet, we find pathetic clinging to France.

Everyone has read the story of Goethe and Frederika, how the great poet, then a student at the Strasburg University, was taken by a comrade to the simple parsonage of Sesenheim, how the artless daughter of the house with her sweet Alsatian songs, enchanted the brilliant youth, how he found himself, as he tells us in his autobiography, suddenly in the immortal family of the Vicar of Wakefield. "And here comes Moses too!" cried Goethe, as Frederika's brother appeared. That accidental visit has in turn immortalised Sesenheim. The place breathes of Frederika. It has become a shrine dedicated to pure, girlish love.

A new line of railway takes us from Strasburg in about an hour over the flat, monotonous stretch of country, so slowly crossed by diligence in Goethe's time. The appearance of the city from this side—the French side—is truly awful: we see fortification after fortification, with vast powder magazines at intervals, on the outer earthworks bristling rows of cannon, beyond, several of the thirteen forts constructed since the war. The bright greenery of the turf covering these earthworks does not detract from their dreadful appearance. Past the vast workshops and stores of the railway station—a small town in itself—past market gardens, hop gardens, hayfields, beech-woods, all drenched with a week of rain, past old-world villages, the railway runs to Sesenheim, alongside the high road familiar to Goethe. We alight at the neat, clean, trim station (in the matter of cleanliness the new *regime* bears the palm over the old), and take the flooded road to the village. An old, bent, wrinkled peasant woman, speaking French, directs us for full information about Frédérique—thus is the name written in French—to the auberge. First, with no little interest and pride, she unhooks from her own wall a framed picture, containing portraits of Goethe, and Frederika, and drawings of church and parsonage as they were. The former has been restored and the latter wholly rebuilt.

As we make our way to the little inn over against these, we pass a new handsome communal school in course of erection. On questioning two children in French, they shake their heads and pass on. The thought naturally arises—did the various French Governments, throughout the period of a hundred and odd years ending in 1870, do much in the way of assimilating the German population of Alsace?

It would not seem so, seeing that up till the Franco-Prussian war the country folk retained their German speech, or at least patois. Under the present rule only German is taught in communal schools, and in the gymnasiums or lycées, two hours a week only being allowed for the teaching of French. At the Auberge du Bouf, over against the church and parsonage, we chat with the master in French about Goethe and Frederika; his womankind, however, only spoke patois. Here, nevertheless, we find French hearts, French sympathies, and occasionally French gaiety.

Unidyllic, yet full of instruction, is the drive in the opposite direction to Kehl. We are here approaching friendly frontiers, yet the aspect is hardly less dreadful. True that cannon do not bristle on the outer line of the triple fortifications; otherwise the state of things is similar. We see lines of vast powder magazines, enormous barracks of recent construction, preparations for defence, on a scale altogether inconceivable and indescribable.

Little wonder that meat is a shilling a pound, instead of fourpence as before the annexation, that bread has doubled in price, taxation also, and, to make matters worse, that trade has remained persistently dull!

A tremendous triple-arched, stone gate, guarded by sentinels, has been erected on this side of the lower Rhine, over against the Duchy of Baden. No sooner are we through than our hearts are rejoiced with signs of peace and innocent enjoyment, restaurants and coffee gardens, family groups resting under the trees. Beyond, flowing briskly amid wooded banks to right and left, is the Rhine, a glorious sight, compensating for so many that have just given us the heartache.

Of Strasburg I will say little. Full descriptions of the new city, for such an expression is no figure of speech, are given in the English, French, and German guide books. The first care of the German Government after coming into possession was to repair the havoc caused by the bombardment, the rebuilding of public buildings, monuments and streets that had been partially or entirely destroyed in 1871. Among these were the Museum and Public Library, the Protestant church, several orphanages and hospitals, lastly, incredible as it may seem, the beautiful octagonal tower of the Cathedral. The incidents of this vandalism have just been graphically described in the new volume of the brothers' Margueritte prose epic, dealing with the Franco-Prussian War, entitled "Les Braves Gens."

I remember writing on the occasion of my first visit to Strasburg, a few years after these events—"There is very little to see at Strasburg now. The Library with its priceless treasures of books and manuscripts, the Museum of painting and sculpture, rich in *chefs d'oeuvre* of the French school, the handsome Protestant church, the theatre, the Palais de Justice, were all completely destroyed by the Prussian bombardment, not to speak of buildings of lesser importance, four hundred private dwellings, and hundreds of civilians killed and wounded by the shells. Nor was the cathedral spared, and would doubtless have perished altogether also but for the enforced surrender of the heroic city."

Since that sad time a new Strasburg has sprung up, of which the University is the central feature. A thousand students now frequent this great school of learning, the professorial staff numbering a hundred. One noteworthy point is the excessive cheapness of a learned or scientific education. Autocratic Prussia emulates democratic France. I was assured by an Alsatian who had graduated here that a year's fees need not exceed ten pounds! Students board and lodge themselves outside the University, and, of course, as economically as they please. They consist chiefly of Germans, for sons of French parents of the middle and upper ranks are sent over the frontier before the age of seventeen in order to evade the German military service. They thus exile themselves for ever. This cruel severance of family ties is, as I have said, one of the saddest effects of annexation. Without and within, the group of buildings forming the University is of great splendour. Alike architecture and decoration are on a costly scale; the vast corridors with tesselated marble floors, marble columns, domes covered with frescoes, statuary, stained glass, and gilded panels, must impress the mind of the poorer students. Less agreeable is the reflection of the taxpayer. This new Imperial quarter represents millions of marks, whilst the defences of Strasburg alone represent many millions more. One of the five facultés is devoted to Natural Science. The Museum of Natural History, the mineralogical collections, and the chemical laboratories have each their separate building, whilst at the extreme end of the University gardens is the handsome new observatory, with covered way leading to the equally handsome residence of the astronomer in charge. Thus the learned star-gazer can reach his telescope under cover in wintry weather. In addition to the University library described above, the various class-rooms have each small separate libraries, sections of history, literature, etc., on which the students can immediately lay their hands. All the buildings are heated with gas or water.

Just beyond these precincts we come upon a striking contrast—row after row of brand-new barracks, military bakeries, foundries, and stores; piles of cannon balls, powder magazines, war material, one would think, sufficient to blow up all Europe. Incongruous indeed is this juxtaposition of a noble seat of learning and militarism only commensurate with barbaric times. A good way off is the School of Medicine. This, indeed, owes little or nothing to the new régime, having been founded by the French Government long before 1870. It is a vast group of buildings, one of which can only be glanced at with a shudder. My friend pointed out to me an annexe or "vivisection department." Here, as he expressed it, is maintained quite a menagerie of unhappy animals destined for the tortures of the vivisector's knife. The very thought sickened me, and I was glad to give up sight-seeing and drop in for half-an-hour's chat with a charming old lady, French to the backbone, living under the mighty shadow of the Cathedral. She entertained me with her experiences during the bombardment, when cooped up with a hundred persons, rich and poor, Jew and Gentile, all passing fifteen days in a dark, damp cellar. Many horrible stories she related, but somehow they seemed less horrible than the thought of tame, timid, and even affectionate and intelligent creatures, slowly and deliberately tortured to death, for the sake, forsooth, of what? Of this corporeal frame man himself has done his best to vitiate and dishonour, mere clayey envelope—so theologians tell us—of an immortal soul!

Strasburg, like Metz, is one vast camp, at the time of this second visit the forty thousand soldiers in garrison here were away for the manoeuvres. In another week or two the town would swarm with them.

I will now say a few words about the administration of the annexed provinces, a subject on which exists much misapprehension.

As I have explained, no liberty, as we understand it, exists for the French subjects of the German Emperor, neither freedom of speech, nor of the press, nor of public meeting are enjoyed in Alsace and the portion of Lorraine no longer French. A rigorous censorship of books as well as newspapers is carried on. Even religious worship is under perpetual surveillance. One by one French pastors and priests are supplanted by their German brethren. A much respected pastor of Mulhouse, long resident in that city and ardently French, told me some years ago that he expected to be the last of his countrymen permitted to officiate. Police officers wearing plain clothes attend the churches in which French is still permitted on Sunday. There is nothing that can be called representative or real parliamentary government. The Stadtholder or Governor is in reality a dictator armed with autocratic powers. He can, at a moment's notice, expel citizens, or stop newspapers. As to administration, it rests in the hands of the State Secretariat or body of Ministers, three in number. There is a pretence at home rule, but one fact suffices to explain its character and working. Of the thirty members forming the local Reichstag, sitting at Strasburg, fifteen are always named by the

Stadtholder himself. This little Chamber of Deputies deliberates upon provincial affairs, all Bills having to pass the Chamber at Berlin and receive the Imperial sanction before becoming law. As to the party of protest in the Reichstag itself, formerly headed by the late Jean Dollfuss, I was assured that it had ceased to exist. Years before, then burdened with the weight of care and years, the great patriot of Mulhouse had said to me, "I no longer take my seat at Berlin. Of what good?" And were he living still, that great and good man, burning as was his patriotism, inextinguishable as was his love for France, would doubtless echo the words I now heard on every lip, "Peace, peace; only let us have peace!"

Whilst at Strasburg German has crowded out French, at Mulhouse I found French still universally spoken. The prohibition of native speech in schools is not only a domestic but a commercial grievance. As extensive business relations exist between the two countries, especially near the frontier, a knowledge of both French and German is really necessary to all classes. Even tourists in Alsace-Lorraine nowadays fare badly without some smattering of the latter language. Hotel-keepers especially look to the winning side, and do their very utmost to Germanise their establishments. Shopkeepers must live, and find it not only advantageous but necessary to follow the same course. Sad indeed is the spectacle of Germanised France! Nemesis here faces us in militarism, crushing the people with taxation and profoundly shocking the best instincts of humanity.

In conclusion I must do justice to the extreme courtesy of German railway and other officials. Many employés of railways and post offices—all, be it remembered, Government officials—do not speak any French at all, especially in out-of-the-way places. At the same time, all officials, down to the rural postman, will do their very best to help out French-speaking strangers with their own scant vocabulary of French words.

My Alsatian hosts, one and all, I found quite ready to do justice to the authorities and their representatives, but, as I have insisted upon before, an insuperable barrier, the fathomless gulf created by injustice, exists between conquerors and conquered. And only last year dining with my hosts of Germanised Lorraine in Paris, I asked them if in this respect matters had changed for the better. The answer I received was categoric—"Nothing is changed since your visit to us. French and Germans remain apart as before."

"East of Paris" has led me somewhat farther than I intended, but to a lover of France, no less than to a French heart, France beyond the Vosges is France still!

Milton Keynes UK
Ingram Content Group UK Ltd.
UKHW040040180324
439604UK00006B/894